WHAT iF...

HOW TO KILL
WORRY AND ANXIETY
BEFORE THEY
KILL *you*

CALEB SUKO

Dovare Publishing

ISBN: 978-0692232095

To my beloved wife, *Christina*.
Thank you for taking care of our
five children and giving me the
time to write!

CONTENTS

PREFACE

When I originally began to write about worry, I never thought it would turn into a book. What you find here had its humble beginnings as a writing assignment in seminary over ten years ago.

After I graduated from seminary, ministry kept me pretty busy for a number of years and most of those seminary papers lay silently deep within my "School Papers" folder on my computer. It wasn't until about two years ago that I rediscovered that paper on worry.

It was actually a word study that was then to be used as a sermon. I can't remember if I had ever preached that sermon back during my seminary days. Nevertheless, the paper grabbed my interest because of some experiences I had just been through. I decided to read through it and study a little further.

I did end up preaching that sermon on worry later; once in our church in Ukraine and again at our home church in Washington State. I found that the more I studied, the more interesting the topic became so I started to write.

The writing process began in late 2012 but I put it down for several long periods of time. It wasn't until early 2014 that I really picked it up again in earnest! It's been a learning process for me. God has taught me much about my own heart and shown me where I lack trust and tend to worry. He's also helped me understand more completely his power over every aspect of my life!

I am grateful that God gave me the chance to write this book. My prayer is that from reading it you will gain a deeper trust in God and a fuller understanding of his care for you!

INTRODUCTION

My firm belief, and what I hope you will see clearly in this book, is that worry is primarily a heart problem that must be treated on the heart level. While this book speaks to practical issues of worry and anxiety, my goal has been to focus on the deeper issues which are the root causes of worry.

Ultimately, all worry stems from faulty thinking that includes a messed up value system, an inadequate understanding of God, and an inflated opinion of self. In order to correct these issues you must look deeply into God's Word and let those truths change you from the inside out.

You'll find that I refer to the Bible often as a source of truth. That's because it is God's revelation to man and, since no one knows you and me better than God, it makes sense to use his Book as the foundation for what we believe and how we behave.

The advice in this book presupposes the truth and perfection of the Bible as God's Word. Much of the advice I give could be used by anyone from any religion, however, I think you'll find at the core one central truth, one defining characteristic that you will not find in any other religion.

What I'm talking about is Jesus, God incarnate, and Savior of all who believe in him.

The truth is that while all the advice you'll find in this book is good, none of it will really have a lasting effect if you don't trust your life with the Author of life -Jesus!

In the end, it's only Jesus who can give you ultimate hope that will kill every worry and all anxiety in your heart. It's only Jesus who can calm your fears and give you a confidence and hope that is eternal.

This is because only Jesus can offer you the solution to your greatest need, which is the need for forgiveness. His forgiveness will change your heart and put you into a right relationship with God. This is the ultimate need of all mankind because, as the Apostle Paul wrote, "All have sinned". (Romans 3:23)

We all share one sad characteristic, we have offended God with our behavior, our thoughts, and our evil intentions. It's not that we're flawed or misguided or mistaken. It's that we are evil, wicked, and sinful. That's the condition of all mankind and only Jesus offers the ultimate solution. He offers forgiveness to all who believe in him.

If you don't believe in Jesus now, I invite you to confess your sin and ask him for forgiveness before you turn the next page! This is the single best thing you can do to kill worry! Jesus died for you and rose from the dead not simply so that you could be free from worry, but more importantly so that you could have the hope of life after death and eternity with Jesus!

> *"Truly, truly, I say to you, whoever hears*
> *my word and believes him who sent me has*
> *eternal life. He does not come into judg-*
> *ment, but has passed from death to life."*
> *(John 5:24)*

Even if you're not ready to believe, I invite you to read with an open mind and an open heart. Allow yourself to be exposed to God's Word and you might be surprised at the results!

CHAPTER

HOW WE START

To be free from worry is a gift; it's the gift of deep, blissful sleep and waking with hope for the day!

Children possess this gift. How can a child go throughout his day without being bothered by the worries and cares of this life? There is a very simple reason - he has perfect trust that his mother and father will provide for his every need. He has never known otherwise. His parents have always clothed him, fed him, comforted him, played with him, sheltered him, and held him close in their arms. Thus, he plays with blissful ease not knowing and not caring that there is a frightfully dangerous world right outside the warm safety of his parents' home.

With maturity comes knowledge of the outside world and responsibility. Often when responsibility comes, so does worry. Let me tell you about how it started in my life.

I'll admit, I tend to be a pretty laid back type of guy, but appearances aren't everything. I can worry too! A couple of years after my wife and I married, we started a small painting business. I bought one of those white utility vans with the ladder racks on top, like the telephone company uses. We lived in Tacoma, Washington, in a part of town that tended to have a lot of drug activity and the crime that goes along with it. Since we were poor seminary students, we could not afford to rent a house with a nice garage where I could park my van. That meant my work van, which was loaded with tools for my painting business, sat out on the street every night.

Honestly, I didn't give it too much thought. I just parked the van on the street in front of our apartment building every night and in the morning it was always there waiting for me. Then one night it happened! They broke the sliding door window and very conveniently removed the contents of my van!

In the morning I got ready for work as usual and headed out the door to find a mess of broken glass on the pavement next to my van. Immediately my stress level shot up; a thousand thoughts invaded my mind and my pulse began to race! Who did this? Where are my tools? How am I going to work today? Where am I going to find the money to replace these things? What's my wife going to say?

I began to ask questions and I began to worry. As a result, I decided to change the way I did a few things. I ordered metal bars for the windows in my van, installed an alarm, and found a nearby storage unit where I could unload most of my valuable tools at night.

Despite the fact that I had made all these changes, I still worried. For the next couple of months my ears were sensitive to the sound of car alarms. I thought every alarm was mine. Several times I got up in the middle of the night to investigate strange noises I had heard outside! Even though my van was technically more secure than it was before the theft, I was now more uneasy about things.

Let's compare my situation with the child I described at the beginning of the chapter. The child doesn't worry because he trusts his parents. However, he also doesn't worry because he lacks knowledge of the dangers of the outside world. Before the break-in, I was like the child.

Yes, I knew that it was theoretically possible for someone to break the window and steal my tools, however, it didn't worry me because I hadn't personally experienced it. The lack of personal experience kept me ignorant of the real danger and allowed me to "sleep like a baby" every night. The problem is that once I went through the experience, it was impossible to go back to the previous state of ignorance.

SLEEPING THROUGH THE STORM

Now let's take a minute and look at Jesus. Here's a guy that could sleep through anything! Remember when Jesus went out on the lake with the disciples? Jesus was sleeping right through a powerful storm that was threatening to sink their boat!

> *And as they sailed he fell asleep. And a*
> *windstorm came down on the lake, and*
> *they were filling with water and were in*
> *danger. And they went and woke him, say-*
> *ing, "Master, Master, we are perishing!" And*
> *he awoke and rebuked the wind and the*
> *raging waves, and they ceased, and there*
> *was a calm.*
> *(Luke 8:23-24)*

There's no question that the disciples were worried in this passage. They didn't gently tap Jesus on the shoulder and say, "Master, if you're not too tired, we could use a little help now." They repeatedly called for him, "Master, Master!" They made the situation look dire, "We're going to die!" They didn't just tell him, they kept telling him!

The disciples couldn't sleep in the storm, but Jesus could!

What was the first thing Jesus said to the disciples after he woke up? You'd think he'd say something like, "Wow, you weren't kidding - that really is a terrible storm!", or maybe he'd say, "Sorry for sleeping, guys; but don't worry - everything will be OK now."

Jesus' response must have shocked the disciples.

He said to them, "Where is your faith?"
And they were afraid, and they marveled,
saying to one another, "Who then is this,
that he commands even winds and water,
and they obey him?"
(Luke 8:25)

After rebuking the wind and the waves, Jesus turns right around and rebukes the disciples for their lack of faith. It was the absence of faith that kept them on edge, didn't allow them to sleep, and caused them to wake Jesus in their desperation.

Babies sleep like babies because they haven't yet experienced all the dangers and problems in life. Their worry-free sleep is what we sometimes call "blissful ignorance". On the other hand, Jesus could sleep despite the fact that he knew there was a storm going on. Jesus could sleep because he had perfect trust in the Father.

You and I don't have the luxury of sleeping in blissful ignorance. If you're old enough to read this book, then you are old enough to know that there are very unpleasant things in this life, things that can keep you up at night.

We've had painful experiences, or heard about others who did, and now we want to avoid them. As our minds struggle to find a way out, to protect us from the dangers of life, we can easily slip into a pattern of worry.

Worry rarely starts suddenly. It begins small and innocent; it's almost hard to recognize at first. We want to look for solutions to possible problems, we want to avoid difficult situations; pain, sickness, and death. This is not wrong. However, our desire to avoid the difficult and distressing things of life can quickly lead to unwarranted fears and a destructive fixation upon the problem and the possible results.

No, worry doesn't usually start suddenly, but when it's not dealt with, it will eventually drag your mind into a deep pit of fear, anxiety, and apprehension. The deeper you go into this pattern of thought, the harder it will be for you to dig yourselves out. It will seem impossible for you not to think about it. Your mind will play through the possibilities over and over again. You become restless, irritated, feeling like you need to do something but not knowing what to do.

Worry infests the mind like maggots, destroying us from the inside out! It paralyzes us with fear, fills us with doubt, and crowds out our ability to think logically and rationally.

There is really only one way out of the pit worry and that is up! Jesus gave us a great example as he slept through the storm. He also pointed us to the only real hope that we have, the only thing that has the ability to rescue us from the depths of our worry!

A CALL FOR FAITH

Jesus reprimanded the disciples for their lack of faith, their failure to believe, their inability to trust. The faith that Jesus was talking about is not a general faith that is often referred to in today's popular culture. It is not faith in some higher good or simply having a positive outlook in life. It most certainly is not faith in yourself, in your abilities or talents. Jesus called us to a faith much higher than ourselves. He called us to believe in the only thing that can actually lift us from our worries and set us on solid ground.

Jesus called for faith in himself!

After all, he had just proved that he was able to calm the storm with his words. Who has power like that?

When it comes down to it, worry is nothing more than your mind desperately looking for a solution to all your problems. When you come to Jesus, you find the ultimate solution. Your tired mind can stop searching; Jesus is the complete answer!

Don't get me wrong, Jesus doesn't promise that when you put your faith in him that he will protect you from all pain and hardship in this life. His promise is much greater! He promises to give you a hope that reaches beyond this momentary life, he guarantees a joy and peace that is much deeper than your temporary struggles. He promises to take your worries upon himself and free you from their weight, but this can't happen until you begin to trust him!

If you're like me, then you have gone through things in your life that could give you reason to worry. You can't un-experience what you have experienced and you can't un-know what you have learned, so that leaves you with only two possibilities. You either choose to make worry an everyday part of your life, or began a life of trust in Jesus and start sleeping well again!

THE ACCEPTABLE SIN

Every culture, every time period, and often every church has a few sins that are considered acceptable. For the patriarchs, polygamy really wasn't that bad. In the New Testament, some churches thought it wasn't a big deal to segregate the rich from the poor. Not so long ago in US history, many churches had no problem segregating blacks from whites.

Today you could make a long list of sins that are acceptable by many in our culture. Worry is one of those acceptable sins.

To be honest, we often don't view worry or anxiety as a sin. Rather than viewing worry as sin rooted in the heart which must be uprooted and destroyed by Jesus, many see it almost as if it were a hobby, a pastime, or just part of their personality. Some people like to read or knit, and others like to ruminate on theoretic situations that could someday make their lives difficult.

To a certain degree, we enjoy worrying. It gives the mind something to do. At first it might even feel like we are solving problems, like we are staying in front of things, or like we are caring for our loved ones. Then we get carried away and soon find that worry has gripped our minds with an uneasy sense of apprehension and doubt that grows with our fixation upon the problem.

WORRY CREATES PROBLEMS

We usually don't realize there is a problem until the strain and tension created by uncontrolled uncertainty in our mind has caused other problems like sleepless nights or even palpitations of the heart. We may begin to see it's negative effects in our family relationships. Anxiety can also keep us from doing things we used to love, such as participating is sports or traveling.

The problems around which worry brews are theoretical and most likely will never come to reality. However, the problems that worry creates are very real! Rarely will we attempt to do anything about worry until the problems which it creates in our life begin to bother us.

What do most people do when these very real complications appear? The first reaction isn't to run to God's Word for help, but rather to treat the outward and physical symptoms. So if you can't sleep, you'll find a whole shelf full of sleep aids at your local pharmacy. If that doesn't work, many turn to alcohol, excessive TV-watching, and many other ways of forcing the mind to temporarily forget its worries.

Then there are the narcotics given to us by the medical establishment as a way to slow the mind and dull the senses. Drugs such as Prozac, Zoloft, Luvox, Xanx and Paxil are used by tens of millions of Americans daily as a means to cope with crippling anxiety, worry, stress, anger, and depression.

We know for certain that these medications affect the processes of the mind and body. We also know that they have many undesirable side effects! What is debatable is whether or not these medications actually help patients get to the root of the problem.

A DIFFERENT PICTURE

When we turn to God's Word, we see a different picture. The Bible clearly teaches not only that worry is sin, but it also gives us guidance on how we should deal with it.

It would have been understandable for many Christians in the early church to struggle with worry; after all, they were under the constant threat of persecution. It didn't take long for all of Jesus' disciples to lose their lives for following Jesus. Paul himself spent much of his time in prison and was beaten by the authorities on several occasions, yet when Paul wrote to the church in Philippi, he told them not to worry!

> *Do not be anxious about anything, but in everything by prayer and supplication with thanksgiving let your requests be made known to God. And the peace of God, which surpasses all understanding, will guard your hearts and your minds in Christ Jesus.*
> *(Philippians 4:6-7)*

Unfortunately, many people are led to believe that their problem is purely a chemical imbalance that can be corrected by ingesting other chemicals which will bring their brain and body into harmony again. By blaming chemical imbalances and treating only the physical results, the whole idea that the underlying cause might be sin is lost.

Kari Scare put it this way,

> I've focused on the chemical imbalance issue as a way to not worry so much (among other reasons). Truthfully, it had a huge impact on changing my thinking. But, the more I focused there, the more I realized its limits. Balancing brain chemicals only took me so far, and I realized at some point there had to be another way for a simpler and more peaceful existence. Only through the Holy Spirit has this existence truly become a reality.
>
> And as long as I keep my focus on Christ, peaceful and simple describe my life. When I don't, my life becomes chaotic and full of worry once again. And this holds true

no matter how perfectly balanced my brain chemicals might be. The Holy Spirit forces us to confront the root cause, and that's where true healing lies.

Kari got it right, but unfortunately, in the minds of many, worry is either something that is passed off as simply a character trait that you can't really change, or a physical defect of the brain that must be treated with medication.

Because we don't see worry as a sin, it is not uncommon to hear people talk about their worry and make passing remarks such as, "Oh, I'm just a worry wart!" or, "I can't help it; I like to worry." They admit their problem, but immediately pass it off as no big deal.

WORRY VERSUS PORNOGRAPHY

Imagine if we applied these statements to other sins. What if you were browsing for movies with a friend and you came across a pornographic film. To your surprise, your friend suggested that you purchase it, and when you ask why, he simply laughs and says, "Oh, I just can't help it; I'm a sexual pervert!"

Even if he were a sexual pervert, he probably wouldn't admit it because that's a sin and he'd be ashamed if you found out. Yet viewing pornography is really not that different from worry.

- Both are sins of the mind.
- Both fantasize about something that is not real.
- Both are patterns of wrong thinking that develop deep thought habits which can be difficult to overcome.
- Both cripple their victims by invading and distracting the mind throughout the day.
- Both can lead to real physical problems.
- Both will lead to relationship problems.
- Both will keep us from pursuing God's will in our life.

Do you remember Jesus' famous "Sermon on the Mount"? (Matthew 5-7) If you read through it, you will find that Jesus speaks about lust in three verses. (Matthew 5:27-29) However, Jesus spends ten verses addressing the problem of worry! (Matthew 6:24-34) That's a good indication that worry really is something we should approach with a serious attitude.

That passage also has one of the clearest statements in the Bible, which prohibits worry in the life of Christians. Jesus simply said it like this:

> *Therefore I tell you, do not be anxious*
> *about your life, what you will eat or what*
> *you will drink, nor about your body, what*
> *you will put on. Is not life more than food,*
> *and the body more than clothing?*
> *(Matthew 6:25)*

Next time you are tempted to brush off worry as an insignificant character trait, you need to stop yourself in your tracks and remind yourself that worry is a sin and, if left unchecked, worry can destroy you just like any sin can.

INVISIBLE SINS

Worry is a sin that most of the time we cannot see or touch. Maybe that is the reason why it is so often brushed off. It's easy to recognize other "big" sins like stealing or drug abuse or sexual immorality. These sins all have a physical aspect to them. They all have something we can point to and say, "There it is!"

There was a group of religious leaders in the Bible called the Pharisees who were experts at pointing out the "big" sins. They had come up with entire systems of how to identify sin. Unfortunately, for their people, the Pharisees where quite good at identifying the sin they could see and touch. However, when it came to recognizing sins of the mind and problems of the heart, they fell short.

Jesus had little patience for the Pharisees. He called them "tombs filled with dead men's bones" (Matthew 23:27). In contrast to the Pharisees, Jesus taught that thoughts and intentions were important because they lie at the root of all we say and do.

> *You have heard that it was said to those of old, "You shall not murder; and whoever murders will be liable to judgment." But I say to you that everyone who is angry with his brother will be liable to judgment; whoever insults his brother will be liable to the council; and whoever says, "You fool!" will be liable to the hell of fire.*
> *(Matthew 5:21-22)*

Jesus raises the bar. Committing murder would be bad for sure, but Jesus says that even being angry is a sin. Anger is a sin of the heart that sometimes can appear in the form of words, however, if left unchecked, can even result in murder.

What Jesus is trying to show us is that all sin really starts in the heart. If we let it go on, it will eventually result in some sort of action in real life. It is vital that we recognize sin while it is still in the heart before it has the chance to expose itself in our actions where it could do real harm!

Just like anger, worry can also manifest itself into real life in a physical way that can be destructive to us and others. We'll talk about that more later.

Maybe you still think worry isn't really that big of a deal or that the best solution is a prescription from your doctor. That's OK, for now; I simply ask that you keep reading.

22

WHAT IS WORRY?

My first job was working for our neighbors pulling weeds. That summer I would make my way across our backyard and then up a little trail through the bushes that led to our neighbor's yard once or twice a week. I spent many hot hours in their flowerbeds, on my knees, meticulously extracting every stray blade of grass or vagrant dandelion.

I didn't particularly enjoy weeding, but I did enjoy the two dollars an hour they would give me! I also felt like I was doing something significant; I was saving the flowerbeds from sure doom! I quickly realized how fast weeds grew. If I didn't come for a week or two, the weeds would already be making a good comeback, they were bigger and their roots were deeper, and they required more of my strength and time to remove!

If left alone for even longer, the weeds would overtake the flowers, occupying every square inch of soil and sucking up the last drops of moisture. The flowers would shrivel up and fall to the ground while the weeds pressed for the sky!

Worry and anxiety are the weeds of the mind and spirit. Do nothing and they will grow! Leave them alone hoping that they will go away, and when you come back, they will be bigger and stronger than before. Eventually they crowd out everything else and do real damage to your spirit!

In the New Testament, Jesus used a similar illustration when he taught his disciples about the destructive nature of worry. In the parable of the soils (Matthew 13:3-9) Jesus explained how worry can completely take over our life, not even leaving room for us to respond to the message of the gospel.

> *Other seeds fell among thorns, and the*
> *thorns grew up and choked them.*
> *(Matthew 13:7)*

Later the disciples asked Jesus to explain this parable to them and this is what he said:

> *As for what was sown among thorns, this is*
> *the one who hears the word, but the cares*
> *of the world and the deceitfulness of riches*
> *choke the word, and it proves unfruitful.*
> *(Matthew 13:22)*

Jesus compares the cares of this life to bushes that invade the space and leave no opportunity for the seed of the gospel to take root in man's heart. He then goes further to talk about how the deceit of possessions and wealth choke out any space that might be left for the seed to grow.

What does Jesus mean by the "cares of life"? The Greek word translated "cares" in Matthew 13:22 is "*merimnah*". It is also often translated as "worries", "cares", or "concerns". It can be used in either a positive or negative sense, but the basic idea is something that distracts or requires attention.

In the context of this parable, the "cares of life" is a general statement that could refer to almost anything in life that turns our attention away from the truth of the gospel.

Jesus was trying to show his disciples how easily the ordinary things of life can become a problem when we allow them to distract us from the most important truths of life. The cares of life can separate us from the very essence of life; they pull us away from the Giver of life and keep us focused on the mundane and superficial aspects of life.

The worries and cares of life are the busyness that consumes us daily. It is waking early with the tasks for the day already on your mind; it is making sure the kids are dressed and fed and out the door for school; it is jumping in the car with coffee in hand and rushing to work; it is receiving a paycheck and paying the bills; it is your regular TV shows and evening news. The worries and cares of life are everything and anything that demand your attention, that never let your mind rest and keep you distracted with the superficial details of getting through another day.

How can we keep those mundane aspects of life from turning our attention away from the gospel? My friend Amy, who is a mother of two young children, shared her thoughts.

> Perhaps the mundane isn't so bad if you've got someone close by who is young enough to listen innocently while you share about God's work amid/throughout the details of the day. We are instructed in Deut. 11:19, "Teach them to your children, talking about them when you sit at home and when you walk along the road, when you lie down and when you get up." Child-like faith matched with our children's endless need to talk/connect seems to provide an abundant amount of opportunity for including Christ in the conversation in our home. TV would rob us of that; so, other than an approved video or Seahawks games, TV is not a contributing member of our family conversations. Our talks with the kids are rich perhaps because of their ages and eagerness to learn. When I'm away from the kids for errands or chores I notice just how precious silence is! So, I suppose, look for people who like to discuss ideas and never stop discussing those ideas with a healthy dose of child-like faith. If you don't have children or unsaved neighbors or co-workers who listen to your glowing report

about the Savior, get a house plant or dog... it's that important. Having someone to talk to about the Lord is one way I stay conscious that He is present! When I'm alone, my thoughts unfortunately center more around myself and the tasks ahead. Can anyone else relate to that? God is still working on me. He is so GOOD!

— Amy Hanson

The things in life that we worry about are not evil by nature, often they are simply tasks that need to be done. The problem is when we allow them to distract us from what is really important, when we allow them to choke out the truth of the gospel in our hearts.

HOW WORRY CHOKES US

It is interesting that even in English the word "worry" seems to have originally communicated the idea of choking.

Mirriam-Webster gives us four meanings for the transitive verb worry.

1. To choke or strangle
2. To harass by tearing, biting, or snapping especially at the throat
3. To assail with rough or aggressive attack or treatment
4. To afflict with mental distress or agitation: make anxious[1]

Do the first three meanings surprise you? They surprised me. Originally the word worry had a very physical meaning. It literally meant to choke or strangle an animal or person. If you think about it, that is an appropriate description for what worry does to us!

Usually when we talk about worry, we give it the fourth meaning,

---

1 http://www.merriam-webster.com/dictionary/worry

"To afflict with mental distress or agitation: make anxious." This type of worry also strangles us. It strangles our thought life by pushing out healthy patterns of thinking. It strangles our faith by overcoming it with anxiety and doubt. It strangles our ability to love and serve others by bogging us down with unfounded fears and suspicions.

Worry can literally strangle us if we are not careful. Shortness of breath is one of the main symptoms of a panic attack, which is ultimately brought on by uncontrolled worry and fear.

The point we need to understand is that worry is destructive. It destroys our spirit as it chokes out the gospel, it also destroys our mind with fear and then it moves on and can even take our physical health from us. Like a parasite, worry invades the mind and takes over. Sometimes it is a slow strangling that can happen over the course of years, and sometimes it can appear from the depths of our heart without warning and send us gasping for air.

While worry may have physical side effects, it always begins in the mind. It is a pattern of destructive thinking that tends to snow-ball, gaining momentum and size if nothing is done to stop it.

I'm convinced that the mind is one of God's greatest gifts to man. God gave man an amazing ability to think and reason, the ability to meditate, analyze, and investigate. When put to the right tasks, these abilities serve us well. They allow us to invent and create, to be industrious, to come up with new solutions, to understand complicated systems, and to engineer better systems.

The same abilities that help us build and create can also tear us down if we are not careful. Worry hijacks our mind's God-given ability to do good. Instead of allowing the mind to create and work for us, worry exhausts our brain power on the hypothetical and theoretical. The thoughts it produces are not useful; they do not help us engage in any constructive activity, but rather hold us back. Worry tangles us in a web of uncontrolled thoughts that pull us further and further from the work God has called us to do.

27

The results of worry are never helpful conclusions or useful advice, but rather more fear, more anxiety, and more theories of how things might go terribly wrong.

IT'S KILLING YOUR BODY

Most of the time, it probably doesn't even cross our minds that doing something mentally could have a negative effect on our body. We can easily forget that the mind is also part of the body God gave us. Our thought habits can have a tremendous effect on our physical health.

Webmd.com gives the following list of physical reactions to a worried state of mind:

- Difficulty swallowing
- Dizziness
- Dry mouth
- Fast heartbeat
- Fatigue
- Headaches
- Inability to concentrate
- Irritability
- Muscle aches
- Muscle tension
- Nausea
- Nervous energy
- Rapid breathing
- Shortness of breath
- Sweating
- Trembling and twitching[2]

OK, maybe that list doesn't seem too bad to you, however, those are just the immediate effects of worry on the body. Over a prolonged period of time, these small problems can turn into big problems.

2 http://www.webmd.com/balance/guide/how-worrying-affects-your-body?page=2

When the excessive fuel in the blood isn't used for physical activities, the chronic anxiety and outpouring of stress hormones can have serious physical consequences, including:

- Suppression of the immune system
- Digestive disorders
- Muscle tension
- Short-term memory loss
- Premature coronary artery disease
- Heart attack[3]

Yes, you read that right - Short-term memory loss and heart attack! Worry really can kill you!

There are also examples in Scripture when fear, worry, and anxiety produced real physical reactions in people. For example, take the time when King Belshazzar saw God's hand write a message on the wall while he was in the middle of a feast. His fear quickly manifested itself physically.

Then the king's color changed, and his
thoughts alarmed him; his limbs gave way,
and his knees knocked together.
(Daniel 5:6)

It literally says that the king's loins were loosed! Fear overwhelmed him and took control of his bodily functions. Worry and fear can do the same to us. The process may not be as sudden as it was for Belshazzar, but if we let it go, eventually worry will take a toll on our body as well as on our mind and spirit.

IT'S KILLING YOU SPIRITUALLY

Worry is a destructive force that invades the mind and damages the body, but it doesn't even stop there! Compulsive worriers

---

3 IBID

find that their own worrying can also damage their relationships. Children with worrying parents learn to despise their parents' constant fears; they also learn to hide information from their worrying mom or dad because of how they will react.

Excessive worry also kills productivity. By nature, worry stops people from doing the normal and necessary things of life. Anxiety can keep a person indoors for years; locked up, a prisoner to their own mind.

I have personally seen how constant fears can kill God-given passions and righteous desires to serve the Lord as a foreign missionary. One of the biggest barriers to missionary service is fear! People dread living in a strange place, dealing with poor medical care, learning a new language. The unfamiliar terrifies many and can keep them chained to their regular life, unable to step out in faith, take a risk and serve God!

If worry doesn't kill us physically, then it certainly kills us spiritually. It gives us thousands of reasons not to serve, not to share Jesus, not to help the needy, not to simply trust that God will take care of us.

More than anything, worry saps us of our faith and depletes us of our trust in God. It leaves us trapped in an endless cycle of anxiety, fear, and apprehension. But there is a way out, there is hope beyond our doubt, there is security beyond our uncertainty. As we look to God's Word together, we will find a clear and well-marked path leading us out of our worry and into the confidence of an almighty, all-knowing God who loves us immensely and cares for us intensely.

4

CONCERN VERSUS WORRY

The year I graduated from high school, I decided to move from under my parents comfortable care in a nice suburban home to the jungles of South America for six months. For me, the thought of living with the natives in palm bark huts, sleeping in a hammock, and trekking through dense jungle sounded exciting. The fact that there could be man-eating snakes, wild natives, and strange jungle diseases made the whole thing sound even more adventurous to me.

Although I looked forward to the adventure and wasn't really too worried about the possible risks, I never stopped to consider what my parents, especially my mom might be thinking. After all, she was sending her barely-eighteen-year-old son half-way around the world to a place where he could very well be eaten by an alligator!

It wasn't until I got back from my six month adventure that it even dawned on me that my mom could have been worried for my safety. Shortly after I came, home the local newspaper wanted to do a story on my trip to the jungle. I willingly gave them an interview and shared how I had gotten lost in the jungle one day, gone on a monkey hunt, and traveled by myself through half of South America. After I shared a bit of my story the reporter turned to my mother and asked, "Didn't you worry that something might happen to your son?" My mother's response was simple; she said, "No, because I knew that God was in control."

As simple as my mother's response was, it's not always so easy in practice. I'm sure she was tempted to worry, to wonder what I was up to, and what possible dangerous situation I might be in so far from her ability to help in any way. This was before the age of the internet, so I couldn't just get on Skype to let her know how things were going. There were weeks between communications.

In situations like these it can be difficult not to worry. When you love and care for someone, it is only natural to be concerned with their well-being.

Although my mother was concerned with my well-being, she didn't let her concern get the best of her and turn into worry or anxiety. The reason she was able to avoid the worry was because she trusted in a God who was greater than she, a God who had the ability to keep me safe when she couldn't.

There is no solid line that divides healthy concern from unhealthy worry, so how do we know when thoughts about the everyday stuff of life have turned from constructive attention into futile worry? After all, we still need to think about the possibilities of the future. We need to make plans, we need to care for our safety, and the safety of others. When done properly, these things are good to think about and create healthy patterns in our mind.

As with any sin, worry is a perversion of something that was originally good. So how do you know when your planning has crossed the line into worry, or when your concern for safety has gone overboard and turned into an unhealthy fear?

I like to use the word "concern" to convey the positive aspects of focusing on a potential problem with the intent to solve it in a beneficial way. On the other hand, I use the word "worry" to convey the negative aspects of fretting over the future. I have found that God's Word also gives us a similar dichotomy.

32

In the New Testament the Greek word *"merimnah"* is often tran slated as *"worry"*. We've already looked at the negative side of that word in chapter three. Now we are going to look at the positive side. When used positively, the same word is often translated "concern".

Let's examine three passages where Paul uses this word to mean something other than worry.

The words in bold are the English translation of the Greek word *"merimnah"*.

> *(32) I want you to be free from **concerns**.*
> *An unmarried man is **concerned** about the*
> *things of the Lord, that is, about how he*
> *can please the Lord.*
> *(33) But a married man is **concerned***
> *about things of this world, that is, about*
> *how he can please his wife,*
> *(34) and so his attention is divided. An*
> *unmarried woman or virgin is **concerned***
> *about the affairs of the Lord, so that she*
> *may be holy in body and spirit. But a mar-*
> *ried woman is **concerned** about the affairs*
> *of this world, that is, about how she can*
> *please her husband.*
> *(1 Corinthians 7:32-34)*[4]

In this chapter, Paul is writing about marriage, and in particular, whether or not singles should marry or stay single. When he tells his readers that he wants them to be "free from concerns" in verse thirty-two, he isn't talking about worry in a negative sense. Rather, he is comparing the life of a married person and and unmarried person. Paul is simply pointing out that once you get married you have to care for your spouse, and this will take your time and attention.

---

4 International Standard Version

However, if you remain single, you have the unique opportunity to completely focus your time and energy on ministry and serving the Lord. Paul is not saying that a married man or woman cannot serve or please the Lord, but rather that they are limited in the time and energy they can give because they have a responsibility to care for their spouse as well.

Thus, "*merimnah*" is used positively in this passage. It communicates the normal care and concern that every married person should exhibit toward their spouse. It also tells us of the attention that an unmarried person can devote to serving the Lord.

> *That there may be no division in the body,*
> *but that the members may have the same*
> *care for one another.*
> *(1 Corinthians 12:25)*

In the verse above, we find "merimnah" in reference to the members of the Body of Christ caring for each other. The point Paul is making is that we ought to be more concerned with serving and loving our brothers and sisters in Christ than with our own personal gain.

> *For I have no one like him, who will be gen-*
> *uinely concerned for your welfare.*
> *(Philippians 2:20)*

In this final verse, Paul speaks of Timothy's deep love and care for the church in Philippi. It is clear that Timothy's genuine interest is a positive quality.

To sum it up, we can say that on the positive side the Greek word "*merimnah*" communicates the following;

- Attention and care for your spouse. (I Cor. 7:32-35)
- Focus on serving the Lord. (I Cor. 7:33-34)
- Love and concern for other members of the church. (I Cor. 12:25, Phil. 2:20)

It's not difficult to see that when "merimnah" is used in a positive way, there it indicates an unselfish and others oriented focus. It shows genuine care and concern for others and for the Lord.

Genuine concern and care for others is an attribute that we must cultivate in our lives. When we begin to exhibit this kind of positive concern, it naturally helps us to overcome the negative aspects of worry and anxiety.

Let's look at the differences between genuine concern and worry.

EIGHT CHARACTERISTICS OF GENUINE CONCERN

1. It is focused on others.
2. It motivates us to serve.
3. It promotes constructive action.
4. It is welcomed by others (most of the time).
5. It is driven by love.
6. Its goal is to help.
7. It strengthens relationships.
8. It is tempered with faith.

SEVEN CHARACTERISTICS OF WORRY

1. It is self-centered.
2. It wastes time and engergy.
3. It is not welcomed by others.
4. It is driven by fear.
5. It doesn't have a goal.
6. It tends to weaken relationships.
7. It overwhelms faith with doubt.

One of the most striking differences between these two uses of the word "*merimnah*" is the fact that genuine concern is always focused on others, but worry is not! In fact, worry is one of the most selfish activities that we can engage in.

At first it might not seem like worry is self-centered; after all, we worry about others. Parents worry about their children. Wives worry about their husbands. Boyfriends worry about their girlfriends, and so on. How could that be self-centered?

When genuine concern crosses over the line and becomes worry, it ceases to be motivated by love and instead is motived by fear. When fear becomes the main motivator, the concern is no longer the well-being of the other person, but rather a desire for control and safety.

The worrier is infatuated with his own fear. His main concern is doing everything possible to assuage the fear that is attacking his mind and heart. The well-being of the other person is really secondary to the pursuit of security for the worrier himself!

In tough times, genuine concern asks, "How can I help you?", but worry asks, "What will I do if something happens to you?" Can you see the shift in focus from "you" to "I"?

How can you know if you have crossed the line from genuine concern into the realm of worry? For starters, I'd suggest taking a look at the seven characteristics of worry that I just gave. If one or more of these factors tend to describe your thinking, then your concern might be turning into worry. If three or more describe you, then you are most likely engaging in worry.

Sometimes it's also helpful to ask ourselves a few good questions to determine whether or not we are worrying. Take fifteen minutes to carefully consider and write out the answers to the following questions:

- Can I stop thinking about it whenever I want?
- Does it keep me up at night?
- Does it keep me or others from doing things that need to be done?
- Is it sometimes hard to concentrate on other things when I need to?

36

CHAPTER

5

QUESTIONS THAT CAN'T BE ANSWERED

Worry strangles its victims in the grip of unanswered questions and false fears.

I like to consider myself a professional question answerer! You see, I have five kids, and if you have children, you probably know where I'm going with this. My kids like to ask questions and they can ask a lot of them!

Here are some questions my wife and I have attempted to answer over the years.

- Do robots have babies?
- Why do we have to go to school?
- Why did God let Adam and Eve sin?
- When am I going to die?

The list goes on! Sometimes their questions are easy to answer. Sometimes their questions stop you in your tracks and make you think about things you've never considered before. Sometimes their questions are just downright ridiculous and I'm at a loss for how to even start answering them.

A few years ago we took a cross country trip in the car to visit some churches that support us as missionaries. As we drove through the flat and "boring" parts of the country, we noticed that our seven-year-old was asking a lot of questions. I quietly looked to my wife and whispered, "Count his questions." Over the course of one hour he asked just over sixty questions!

That's sixty questions that we had to find answers to! Here is what we noticed - answering questions takes energy. In fact it takes so much energy out of me that sometimes I have to tell my kids to take a break from asking question so that my mind can have a little rest!

Not all questions take the same amount of energy to answer. If I ask you what 1+1 equals, you hardly need to blink because you already know the answer. However, let's take a harder question, say 11+15-7x3. OK, now you had to stop and think for a minute. Or maybe you were too lazy and you just kept reading because you thought the answer wasn't really that important or I'd give you the answer later. If you really want to know the answer, it's five!

We know that math problems should have answers; they make sense, but let's take a different type of question. What if I were to ask you one of the following?

- Why do one-year-olds get cancer?
- Why does God allow rape of innocent little girls?
- Why does the first world struggle with obesity while the third world struggles with starvation?

Did you answer those questions yet? Probably not, and if you did I'd question your answers! These types of questions make us feel uncomfortable. They play with our understanding of the world. They don't fit well with some things we know and believe. We struggle when we search for answers and it drains us. Try to answer these types of questions for long enough and you'll go away feeling tired mentally, emotionally, and quite possibly physically!

These are exactly the kind of questions worry asks us! Worry bombards us with:

- Will I be OK?
- Why is he so late; did something happen?
- What will they say?
- What will I do?

And the big one: "What if..."

These questions create tension in our brain. It's impossible to answer them all. Often, even if we do answer some of them, worry will immediately replace the answered questions with ten more unanswered questions. We deceive ourselves into thinking that if we only knew the answer to the immediate question, our worry would vanish.

Unanswered questions drain our strength quicker than any other kind of question. Deep inside we know that there are millions of possible answers. As we worry, our mind sifts through those millions of possible answers one-by-one. It's a never-ending process that can overshadow everything else in our life.

"WHAT IF..."

This is the granddaddy of all the questions worry asks. In reality, "What if..." has some merit to it. It's a great question to ask when you are creating something. If you've ever gone through the process of building a house then you probably experienced the good side of "What if..."

- What if we made this room bigger?
- What if we moved the doorway?
- What if we painted the house yellow?

Those are good questions to ask because they help you decide how to create something that will be useful and meet your needs. In this sense, "What if..." deals with reality. You really are building a house and you really do have some choices to decide on. However, those choices are limited by your budget. You're not deciding between building a multimillion dollar mansion or a shack. There are other factors that limit your choices like the overall the design of the house, and whether or not it is even structurally possible.

Finally, the good kind of "What if..." is part of the creative process. This type of thinking is healthy for the mind. It allows us to use our imaginations to create something that will be beautiful, practical, comfortable, safe, and useful.

RISK MANAGEMENT

"What if..." can also be asked in a positive way to minimize dangers. When done correctly this is called "risk management". Many worriers think they are just good risk managers, but this is far from the truth. Let's take a look at the difference between risk management and worry.

True risk management is a science based on solid research and real data. Worry is a thought habit based on our fears and fantasy.

Risk management assesses potential risks based on real numbers and past experiences. Worry doesn't assess anything; it just dwells on endless possibilities.

Risk management implements a plan that helps people successfully and safely complete their projects. Worry doesn't have a plan; it just keeps you from doing what you need to do.

Risk management does its job and moves on. Worry never stops running the possibilities through your mind like a broken record.

In contrast to risk management worry asks a completely different type of "What if...".

Worry uses "What if…" as an excuse not to do something that we are uncomfortable with. Let's look at a great example from the book of Exodus.

Do you remember Moses at the burning bush? God asked Moses to go back to Egypt and lead his people out of slavery. It was a big task and, at first, Moses wasn't comfortable with it.

> *Then Moses said to God, "If I come to the*
> *people of Israel and say to them, 'The God*
> *of your fathers has sent me to you,' and*
> *they ask me, 'What is his name?' what shall*
> *I say to them?"*
> *(Exodus 3:13)*

Can you see what Moses is really doing here? He is asking a "What if…" question. We could put it this way; "***What if*** they ask me who sent me?" Honestly, I don't think Moses was as concerned with the answer to his question as he was in finding an excuse to get out the task God had given him.

God answers Moses' "What if…" in the following verse:

> *God said to Moses, "I AM WHO I AM." And*
> *he said, "Say this to the people of Israel, 'I*
> *AM has sent me to you.'"*
> *(Exodus 3:14)*

This is more than just a name to separate God from others. "I AM WHO I AM" is a description of God's nature. It is theology in its purest form. The truest truth of all truths is simply this -God exists! He didn't start existing and he will never stop existing, he simply IS!

The fact that God is, means he is uncreated, as a result, he alone has the ability to act completely independent of creation. Now pay close attention because this is where it gets really important! God never asks "What if…" because God is!

Let me explain what I mean.. "What if..." is nothing more than our desire to know every variable and every possible outcome of any given situation. When we ask that question, we prove that we are not God, because if we were God, we would know the outcome.

Asking "What if..." is our incompetent attempt to play God. We don't feel comfortable when we don't know all the answers, when we feel like things may be out of our control, or when we are unsure if everything will be "OK". We mistakenly think that if we could answer all the "What ifs" we would feel better and more confident about the situation!

What does God want us to do? God wants us to forget the "What if..." and instead focus on "What is!" God wants us to focus on the truth that we know rather than the millions of theoretical outcomes that we couldn't possibly know.

This is exactly what God does with Moses in Exodus chapter three. When Moses brings up the "What if...", God turns it right around and tells Moses "What is!" - God is! There is no simpler truth, and when we comprehend the utter honesty of God's existence, our "What ifs" tend to vanish. They dissipate in the light of a God who IS, a God who IS all knowing, a God who IS all powerful, a God who IS with us, a God who IS loving!

CHAPTER

6

THE RISK OF FAITH

As a kid growing up in Western Washington, our family liked to get out to the mountains in the summer. All eight of us kids would pile into our two-toned, twelve-passenger 1981 Chevrolet Beauville van. My dad had customized it with a table in the back. We enjoyed sitting at the table, playing games while we cruised down the highway.

Once we hit the mountain, we'd usually stop playing our games and start staring out the windows at the scenery. Our van wasn't particularly nimble on narrow, curvy mountain roads, but my dad always managed to get us there and back safely.

There's something about being in a big van loaded with kids that makes the whole experience ten times more exciting than if we were in a regular car with a couple of boring adults. The higher we climbed, the greater the excitement.

I enjoyed looking straight down out of the window over the edge of the cliff as my dad eked the car around another turn. I'd purposely sit on the side of the drop-off so I could get a better view.

However, for one of my brothers, the experience wasn't quite as enjoyable. While I had my face squished against the window, he'd be laying on the floor of the van pleading with my dad to slow down. Of course my dad got a little thrill out of driving just a little closer to the edge than was needed.

My brother didn't like the unnecessary risk, and instead of looking at the scenery, he preferred to spend that part of the trip as close to the ground as possible. I'm not sure if he thought that bringing his weight closer to the ground would stabilize the van, or if he was just trying to avoid looking at the drop-off. I suppose it was a little of both; although, I suspect that him lying on the floor didn't really make anyone safer.

Worry has a similar effect on us. We think that when we engage in worrying that we are somehow "fixing" the problem or making things safer. In reality, we are doing little more than dropping to the floor in hopes that if we can't see the edge of the cliff, then maybe it's not really there.

What my brother did was ironic. In his quest, for safety he unfastened the one thing that was keeping him safe - his seat-belt! His worry led to a compromise and actually put him in more danger than if he were to have remained in his seat with his seat-belt fastened.

Whether you like it or not, worry that goes unchecked will always lead you to compromise your values. This happens when you are faced with the risk of faith. Maybe you didn't think about it before, but faith always has an element of risk in it.

Faith is believing a certain truth that is communicated to us by another person. Here's a simple illustration. Let's say you decide to ride with me in my car to the store. You've never ridden in my car before. You've never even seen me drive a car before, but I tell you, "Don't worry, I have a driver's license; I'm a good driver and I know the way." When you believe what I just told you, that is faith; when you get in the car with me, that is risk.

The truth is, you can't be 100% sure that everything I'm telling you is true; however, you take my word for it. You make a quick evaluation of the situation and decide that it's reasonable to think that I'm a trustworthy person. Then you step out in faith by stepping into my car, and in doing so, you also take a risk. After all, you don't know everything; it's possible I wasn't telling you the truth; it's possible that we'll get into a car accident on the way to the store.

THE RISK GOD WANTS YOU TO TAKE

You might think my illustration is unfair because we can be 100% sure of everything God tells us. You're right, we can have total confidence in God; however, sometimes God asks us to do things that are risky.

Making a righteous decision often brings with it some type of risk. Let's look at a few examples.

- Honestly paying your taxes brings the risk that you might not have enough money to pay other bills.
- Sharing the truth of Jesus with others brings the risk of ridicule and possible persecution in many countries.
- Abstaining from sex before marriage brings with it the risk of remaining single for the rest of your life.
- Picking up your family and moving to another country to serve God brings a myriad of risks.

Without risk, faith is hardly faith at all. If there really were nothing to it, and faith consisted of no more than acknowledging a simple fact in your head, then there would be a lot more believers in this world.

WORRY LEADS TO COMPROMISE

True faith always results in some sort of righteous action. These actions often bring a certain level of risk with them. If we feel our faith is not worth the risk, we will compromise our faith every time.

True faith looks beyond worry to the truth that it believes in. An honest faith is so grounded in truth, that risk takes a backseat. On the other hand, worries' greatest fear is risk. Worry sees potential for danger in almost everything and will avoid that risk at any cost. Unfortunately, the cost of avoiding perceived risk is often the compromise of our morals.

Let's take a look at one example of how worry can lead to compromise from the book of Genesis.

Abraham is known as the great patriarch of Jews and of Christians. He was a man of faith who simply believed what God told him, yet he was also human, and, like you and I, he sometimes stumbled in his faith.

> *When he was about to enter Egypt, he said*
> *to Sarai his wife, "I know that you are a*
> *woman beautiful in appearance, and when*
> *the Egyptians see you, they will say, 'This*
> *is his wife.' Then they will kill me, but they*
> *will let you live. Say you are my sister, that*
> *it may go well with me because of you, and*
> *that my life may be spared for your sake."*
> *(Genesis 12:11-13)*

Abraham was afraid of the risk. What would happen if the Egyptians wanted to take his wife from him? Abraham assumed that they'd kill him. In order to avoid such danger, he compromised his commitment to honesty and to his wife! He decided not to tell the Egyptians that Sarai was his wife.

I guess he thought it would be better to let his wife marry someone else rather than to show his love as a husband by standing up for her, even if that meant he should die for it.

Did Abraham correctly analyze the situation? Well, yes and no. Abraham got two things right. Sarai was beautiful and it was possible that Abraham could lose his life over her. I'm pretty sure that if the Pharaoh had wanted to, he'd have no problem taking out Abraham and claiming Sarai for himself.

So where did Abraham go wrong?

His first mistake was assuming that his own life was more important than the moral standard given by God. The truth is that if Abraham had not lied, he may have lost his life, but that's OK! No one's life is more important than God's standard.

You and I do the same thing all the time. We might compromise our honesty on our taxes because we believe the money we gain is more significant than the standard we have compromised.

We compromise our opportunities to communicate the message of Jesus to our neighbors because we believe that losing face, being ridiculed, or looking stupid is worse than ignoring Jesus' command in Matthew 28:19 to make disciples!

The mistake we make is thinking that we are either gaining or safeguarding something that is more important than God's clear command.

Abraham's second mistake was to misjudge God's ability. Yes, it was a risky situation, but guess what? God can handle that risk! No pharaoh, no king, no president is beyond God's control. God knows your situation; he knows the risk you might be taking in order to uncompromisingly hold to your faith.

God can and often does protect and reward those who take risks for him. He took Joseph from a prison to a palace, he granted Esther the safety of her people, he shut the mouths of lions for Daniel, and the list goes on.

I'm not saying that God will guarantee your safety in every circumstance. I'm just saying that he has the ability, and if he sees fit to protect you from danger, he will. The problem is, we rarely take into account God's abilities when we weigh the risks of a given situation.

47

We have a responsibility to remain faithful to truth no matter what the risk. God calls us to take righteous risks in dangerous situations. We must boldly step through those doors realizing that God's truth is far more valuable than anything we might consider trading it in for; even our life.

TOO CONCERNED TO WORRY ABOUT THE RISK

The Apostle Paul, who wrote many of the books in the New Testament, gives us a great example of how true faith overcomes the worry of potential risks in our life.

The Jewish leaders were so upset with Paul for his conversion and bold preaching of the Gospel that they devised a plan to murder him if he returned to Jerusalem. When Paul decided to go back to Jerusalem, where he was a wanted man, some of his closest friends thought he was crazy. They warned him that he would be apprehended by the Jews and tied up. Paul must have shocked them with his response when he said,

> *Then Paul answered, "What are you do-*
> *ing, weeping and breaking my heart? For*
> *I am ready not only to be imprisoned but*
> *even to die in Jerusalem for the name*
> *of the Lord Jesus."*
> *(Acts 21:13)*

Paul believed in the mission God had given him, and he had faith in the one who sent them. Paul went despite the risks! Paul also understood the risk of faith and he put it this way.

> *But if there is no resurrection of the dead,*
> *then not even Christ has been raised. And*
> *if Christ has not been raised, then our*
> *preaching is in vain and your faith is in*
> *vain. We are even found to be misrepresent-*
> *ing God, because we testified about God*
> *that he raised Christ, whom he did not raise*

48

if it is true that the dead are not raised. For
if the dead are not raised, not even Christ
has been raised. And if Christ has not been
raised, your faith is futile and you are still
in your sins. Then those also who have
fallen asleep in Christ have perished. If in
Christ we have hope in this life only, we are
of all people most to be pitied.
(1 Corinthians 15:13-19)

If Jesus really isn't the Messiah, then those who have chosen to follow him should be pitied more than anyone else. They have wasted their faith. They have wasted their life on something that gave them a false hope. They have endured trials and pain for a fake. That's the risk of faith in Jesus!

That's a big risk. That's a risk that many are not willing to take. Most people would rather play it "safe" rather than risking their temporary pleasure by putting their faith in Jesus.

True faith pushes aside the barriers that risk builds in our minds. It affirms a truth so deeply, that it is willing to risk all to put that truth into action. Faith put into action brings with it a completely new set of rules. The person who lives by faith does not dwell on all the risk factors. Instead, the truth of what they believe is the primary motivating factor. The more significant the truth, the greater its ability to push beyond risk and call for action in all circumstances.

Let's think about Paul again. Without any doubt, Paul was motivated by his belief that Jesus was God, the Messiah, and the Savior of mankind. This belief motivated him to do some very risky things!

When Paul wrote a letter to his protégé, Timothy, he described his motivation like this:

Remember Jesus Christ, risen from the
dead, the offspring of David, as preached in

my gospel, for which I am suffering, bound
with chains as a criminal. But the word
of God is not bound! Therefore I endure
everything for the sake of the elect, that
they also may obtain the salvation that is
in Christ Jesus with eternal glory.
(2 Timothy 2:8-10)

And believe me, Paul did endure hardships! When he wrote a letter to the church in the city of Corinth, he listed some of the trials he had experienced.

Five times I received at the hands of the
Jews the forty lashes less one. Three times
I was beaten with rods. Once I was stoned.
Three times I was shipwrecked; a night
and a day I was adrift at sea; on frequent
journeys, in danger from rivers, danger
from robbers, danger from my own peo-
ple, danger from Gentiles, danger in the
city, danger in the wilderness, danger at
sea, danger from false brothers; in toil and
hardship, through many a sleepless night,
in hunger and thirst, often without food, in
cold and exposure.
(2 Corinthians 11:24-27)

Have you ever been whipped or stoned? Would it worry you if you thought that might happen if you shared the gospel with someone?

Somehow, that type of risk didn't worry Paul. He was too concerned with the task he had been given and the truth he lived by to be worried about whether or not he might be whipped, beaten, stoned, shipwrecked, or worse!

Do you want to know what Paul was really concerned about? He tells the Corinthian church in the very next verse.

*And, apart from other things, there is
the daily pressure on me of my anxiety
for all the churches.
(2 Corinthians 11:28)*

Paul's biggest concern was the spiritual well-being of the churches he had started. The word translated "anxiety" in 2 Corinthians 11:28 comes from the Greek word "*merimnah*", which we discussed in chapter four.

Paul was genuinely concerned for these churches. We know that he prayed for them, wrote them letters, visited them, taught them, and sent others to pastor them. This all indicates that Paul's concern was the good type. It was the type of worry that offered true help and promoted action.

THE "DON'T WORRY BE HAPPY" MYTH

In 1988 singer/songwriter Bobby McFerrin wrote a song that hit the top of the charts called "Don't worry, be happy".

The song had a fun relaxed island feel and the words went like this:

Here's a little song I wrote
You might want to sing it note for note
Don't Worry, Be Happy
In every life we have some trouble
But when you worry you make it double
Don't Worry, Be Happy
Ain't got no place to lay your head,
somebody came and took your bed
Don't Worry, Be Happy
The landlord say your rent is late,
he may have to litigate
Don't Worry, Be Happy
Ain't got no cash, ain't got no style,
ain't got no gal to make you smile
Don't Worry, Be Happy
Cause when you worry your face will frown
and that will bring everybody down
Don't Worry, Be Happy[5]

5 http://bobbymcferrin.com/dont-worry-be-bobby

Many viewed Bobby's advice as a simple solution for their worries. All they had to do was replace their worry with a smile and a happy disposition and everything would be OK! It seems so easy, but there's a problem!

Bobby McFerrin doesn't give you any basis for a worry free life; the most he can come up with is that worry will make your trouble double, and in that he's right. But what's going to happen when someone does take your bed or your landlord evicts you? How are you going to deal with that? Certainly a smile and a positive disposition aren't going to convince your landlord to let you live rent-free!

The philosophy, and even the words, behind McFerrin's song come from a famous Indian mystic called Meher Baba, who was noted for signing his communications with "Don't worry, be happy."[6]

Meher Baba also considered himself to be god incarnate. He voluntarily spoke no audible words for the last forty-four years of his life and he taught that reality is an illusion created by our imagination. Maybe that's why he could simply ask his followers not to worry and instead be happy; after all, if reality isn't real, then your problems aren't real either!

Unfortunately Meher Baba's belief that reality was an illusion didn't stop him from being involved in two serious car accidents that left him crippled and in pain for the rest of his life!

IMPOTENT ADVICE

The problem with the "Don't worry, be happy" philosophy is that it's impotent and incapable of delivering on its promise. Its like telling someone who's hungry to be satisfied, but not giving them any food; or telling someone who's shivering from the cold to be warm, but not giving them warm clothing.

---

6 http://en.wikipedia.org/wiki/Don't_Worry,_Be_Happy

Sure, you can temporarily put a smile on your face, pull yourself up by the bootstraps, and act like everything is going to be OK, but that won't change reality, and eventually you'll find yourself flat on your face again.

Meher Baba's philosophy simply trains us to be good at ignoring reality; it gives us no promise to hold onto, no truth to anchor ourselves with. If your life consists only of reading books on a quiet beach under the shade of a palm tree, then maybe it's a good philosophy for you! However, if you're like the rest of us, then you can't afford to ignore reality and the problems that call for your attention on a daily basis.

EVERYTHING IS GOING TO BE FINE. REALLY?

Christina and I experienced this first hand about ten years ago when our one-year-old son was diagnosed with cancer. It was spring of 2004, and life was moving along at a hurried pace. I was busy with my seminary studies, running a small painting business, serving as an intern pastor at our church, and raising a growing family. We could almost feel the wind in our hair as life accelerated forward, and we were doing all we could to hang on.

Then the doctor told us, "Your son has a large malignant tumor in his abdomen." Our life came to a halt! Suddenly we were standing at the edge of a small bed, watching the body of our little boy give way to cancer.

Shortly after we received that news, I remember talking with of one my customers. When I told him about the diagnoses, his response was, "Don't worry, everything is going to be fine." His words bit into my soul, and I heard a silent voice in my head sharply respond, "Really, really? How do you know that?"

I cringed on the inside, but on the outside I responded with a half-smile and slight nod of my head. I knew that he was just trying to say something nice, something that would encourage me and give me a little hope. Or maybe it was his effort to fill the awkward silence after I had finished telling him that my one-year-old boy had just been diagnosed with cancer.

I thought it would be rude to let on that I didn't believe his optimism, so instead of asking him how he knew everything would be alright and why he was so confident that my son would be healed, I carefully moved the conversation on to how well the hospital staff was taking care of my boy and how they had these amazing new technologies for treating cancer.

Cancer is a heavy word. It drops into your soul like a wrecking ball and crushes hope. Our hope that Mishael would survive cancer was expressed to us by his doctor in percentages. The somewhat-high success rate of 80% didn't seem comforting! All we could think about was the 20% chance that we could lose our son before his second birthday.

Before we could finish wiping the tears from our cheeks, we had the Bible open in a desperate search for hope. What we found was that in the same way cancer kills hope, there is another word that revives it!

JESUS!

Blessed be the God and Father of our Lord Jesus Christ! According to his great mercy, he has caused us to be born again to a living hope through the resurrection of Jesus Christ from the dead, to an inheritance that is imperishable, undefiled, and unfading, kept in heaven for you.
(1 Peter 1:3-4)

The hope that Jesus gave us didn't express itself in percentages, but rather with words like imperishable, undefiled, unfading, and living.

The hope that Jesus gave us didn't make empty promises in ignorance just to make us feel good, it was the full promise of the all-knowing and all-powerful God. The hope that Jesus gave us didn't depend on advanced medical technologies and well-trained doctors; it depended only on the sacrifice of a loving Savior.

No one could give us a guarantee that our child would survive cancer, but Jesus gave us the confidence that even if our son didn't make it, there was hope that we would see him again. Our hope in Jesus' ability to give life beyond the grave gave us the strength we needed to live this side of the grave.

THE DIFFERENCE

Now that's a hope and assurance that is far different from the empty words in Bobby McFerrin's song, "Don't Worry Be Happy". The difference is drastic! One teaches you to ignore reality and force out worry by putting a smile on your face, the other faces the sometimes gruesome reality of life and says, "Jesus has got this; you don't have to face it alone, he will be with you and he will provide hope beyond this life!"

Maybe you're wondering what happened to our son. Thankfully, God saw fit to heal him through the work of doctors, nurses, and medical technology! Today he is healthy growing twelve-year-old boy. We are glad that he came through cancer and is healthy now, but we also know that even if he didn't survive, Jesus was still our hope whether in life or in death.

If you've got your trust placed in Jesus, then you really don't have any reason to worry! Life will not always be roses, and you may not always be be comfortable, but you can always be confident in Jesus' ability to bring you through!

8

CONQUER YOUR FEARS AND FACE THE FACTS

Have you ever seen any of the "Jaws" movies? If you have, then you probably just shuddered a bit as your read the word "Jaws." It immediately brings to mind footage of a Great White Shark attacking unsuspecting victims who are enjoying a relaxing swim. It's not something you want to watch just before your summer vacation at the beach. In fact, I'm pretty sure that Steven Spielberg has prevented millions of people from enjoying a nice swim!

I remember watching "Jaws" when I was about ten years old. The following summer, I was a little timid even to get into my aunt's backyard pool. I had an eerie feeling that maybe, just maybe, a shark could be lurking at the bottom of that pool, waiting for me to stick my foot in.

Despite my fear, I would always eventually get in the pool. Why? Because I could see the bottom and there was no shark there!

Fear is an overwhelming emotion that can easily overtake our mind and dictate our actions. Worry and fear go well together. They play off each other and exponentially increase if they are not stopped.

Almost all worries are related to a fear. Your worry about money stems from a fear that you won't have enough to pay the bills. Your worry about health comes from a fear that you might get sick. Your worry about your son or daughter arises from a fear that they might be in danger.

It's a vicious circle; the more you worry, the more you fear, and the greater your fear, the more you tend to worry! What can you do to stop this worry/fear cycle?

The answer is simple - face the facts!

For me, that meant staring at the bottom of my aunt's pool to make sure there weren't any sharks waiting for me. Once I convinced myself that there were no sharks, the fear melted away.

The thing about fear is that it is rarely based upon truth; like worry it finds its home in the hypothetical and theoretical. Assumptions, imagination, and blind guesses are fear's ally! In order to eliminate it, we need to bring our minds out of the cloud of speculation and back to the solid ground of truth.

The reality is that we usually can't see the bottom of the pool. We can't prove 100% that there are no sharks, because life doesn't happen in the confines of a small, clean backyard pool. The waters of life can be dark, and sometimes the waves are over our head; we usually don't know exactly what's in those waters.

Nevertheless, there are a few facts that we need to know and remind ourselves of. These truths, if understood and believed will eliminate fear from your life!

GOD KNOWS YOU

You may think that your spouse, your parents, or your best friend know you well, and maybe they do, but it's nothing compared to how well God knows you! God knows you better than you know yourself, and there is something comforting in that fact.

David describes God's knowledge of himself this way,

> *O LORD, you have searched me and known*
> *me! You know when I sit down and when I*
> *rise up; you discern my thoughts from afar.*
> *You search out my path and my lying down*
> *and are acquainted with all my ways. Even*
> *before a word is on my tongue, behold, O*
> *LORD, you know it altogether. You hem me*
> *in, behind and before, and lay your hand*
> *upon me. Such knowledge is too wonderful*
> *for me; it is high; I cannot attain it.*
> *(Psalm 139:1-6)*

In this piece of beautiful poetry, David focuses on God's detailed knowledge of us. He uses words and phrases like understand, scrutinize, familiar, know completely to describe God's intimate knowledge of everything about us; he even knows what we think before we think it!

God doesn't just know about you, he knows you! He knows what you do and he knows how you think. Why is this comforting? If God knows everything about you, then he also knows all potential dangers, and nothing can catch him off guard.

David was overwhelmed by this kind of knowledge, but I don't think that it was just the fact that God knew a lot about him. This description of God's knowledge indicates that these facts about David's life are much more than raw data to God!

GOD CARES FOR YOU

God's intimate knowledge of David pointed to the fact that God loved and cared for David. Think about it, those who know you best care for you the most, and no one knows you better or more than God.

Jesus also reminds us of God's care for us, expressed in his knowledge of us.

> *Are not two sparrows sold for a penny? And*
> *not one of them will fall to the ground apart*
> *from your Father. But even the hairs of your*
> *head are all numbered. Fear not, therefore;*
> *you are of more value than many sparrows.*
> *(Matthew 10:29-31)*

Realizing that someone loves you and cares for you is encouraging and empowering. I've had tough days both in business and in ministry. On many occasions I've come home feeling beat up, tired, and discouraged. Then I see the smiling face of my wife, and my spirit changes. I've often told Christina that just the knowledge that she loves me and cares for me often gives me the strength that I need.

How much more encouraging and empowering is it to know that the Creator God knows you and cares for you? When fear, discouragement or anxiety strike, this is the foundation we need to come back to. This is what we can know for sure!

Peter puts it so clearly and simply!

> *...casting all your anxieties on him, because*
> *he cares for you.*
> *(1 Peter 5:7)*

GOD IS WITH YOU

Not only does God know you and care for you, but his Spirit is always with you. You can not flee from him, run away from him, or hide from him. God is there wherever you are. That is something you can place your full confidence in!

Everything seems just a bit scarier when you're alone than when you have someone at your side. However, even when there are thousands of people nearby, you can still feel alone. That loneliness will often lead to more fear and more worry.

It's easy to get caught up in our loneliness and start believing the lie that we must do everything on our own and everything depends upon our abilities and strengths.

Again we turn to David's writing in Psalm 139. After he described God's amazing knowledge of everything about him, David shows how God is always present.

> *Where shall I go from your Spirit? Or where*
> *shall I flee from your presence? If I ascend*
> *to heaven, you are there! If I make my bed*
> *in Sheol, you are there! If I take the wings*
> *of the morning and dwell in the uttermost*
> *parts of the sea, even there your hand shall*
> *lead me, and your right hand shall hold me.*
> *If I say, "Surely the darkness shall cover*
> *me, and the light about me be night," even*
> *the darkness is not dark to you; the night*
> *is bright as the day, for darkness is as light*
> *with you.*
> *(Psalm 139:7-12)*

Take heart because you're not alone! You're not alone when you have bills to pay, you're not alone when you're struggling with cancer, you're not alone when you lose your job, you're not alone when your child is being rebellious, your not alone in your depression, discomfort, or pain!

Knowing that we are not alone, but that God is with us every step of the way, gives us the courage we need to take a forward step of faith and to dive into the water, even if we can't see the bottom!

GOD IS ABLE TO MEET YOUR NEEDS

God's knowledge and care are comforting, but we need more

than that; we need to know God's ability! All too often, we under-estimate what God can do. Our weak view of God cripples our faith and allows for worry and doubt to creep in.

Sometimes we need to remind ourselves that God is the Creator of everything!

For by him all things were created, in
heaven and on earth, visible and invisible,
whether thrones or dominions or rulers
or authorities—all things were created
through him and for him.
(Colossians 1:16)

Isaiah describes God's abilities in poetic form.

Who has measured the waters in the hollow
of his hand and marked off the heavens
with a span, enclosed the dust of the earth
in a measure and weighed the mountains in
scales and the hills in a balance?
(Isaiah 40:12)

This same God can and will provide for our needs.

And my God will supply every need
of yours according to his riches
in glory in Christ Jesus.
(Philippians 4:19)

When you compare your fear to God's ability, it's really no match; God will come out the victor every time and our fears will vanish.

GOD IS ABLE TO GIVE YOU PEACE

Fear stirs up the heart and gives it no rest. You can't have fear and peace at the same time. In today's world, peace is sought after by nearly everyone but it is rarely found. Some have even called

64

political peace a time to reload, unfortunately, that statement is more accurate than I'd like to admit!

The peace that God offers us through Jesus is unique. Unlike political peace, it's not a time to reload! Jesus satisfies our greatest need for peace on the heart level. He allows us to have peace with God.

Peace I leave with you; my peace I give to you. Not as the world gives do I give to you. Let not your hearts be troubled, neither let them be afraid.
(John 14:27)

Paul tells us in Ephesians 2:14 that Jesus is our peace. He stands between us and God because he satisfied God's judgement on our sin by providing a perfect sacrifice when he died on the cross. As a result, we can have peace with God when we trust in Jesus' work on our behalf.

No one can take that kind of peace away from you and no fear can stand against it. It's a peace that will be with you for eternity!

9

GIVE OVER THE CONTROL

I have five children, and as I write this, the youngest is four years old, which means that Christina and I have already gone through the toddler experience five times!

It's always interesting to watch how a child develops during those early years. As they begin to talk, they take on a personality of their own. They also begin to exhibit the desire for independence.

All of a sudden, I find that the little baby who could do absolutely nothing for himself wants to feed himself, clothe himself, and make his own decisions. While one of my goals for my children is to teach them to live independently from me, I'm really not looking to have them move out on their own at two years old!

I can't count the number of times I've wrestled with my two-year-old son or daughter, as I struggled to get them dressed. It's really a fight for independence and control! The usual complaint is, "I can do it myself!" and sometimes it's, "I don't want to wear that!" After all, why shouldn't I let my toddler wear rubber boots and an over-sized t-shirt to church on Sunday morning?!

Here's the irony, those simple tasks that I know they can do on their own, they don't want to do. When I ask a two-year-old to pick up his toys, there's a good chance he'll lay on the floor crying for the next thirty minutes. He'll say that it's too hard and he needs help and that you're a cruel parent to even demand such a thing!

It's really just human nature; we want control without responsibility! We want to determine our destiny as long as others are willing to fix our mistakes.

But what happens when we try to control things that we were not designed to control? We make things a lot harder for ourselves because we end up struggling with God, just like my children would struggle with me while donning a pair of Sunday breeches.

THE LIE OF CONTROL

Too often we are tempted to believe the lie that if we did it our way, things would be better. Too often we are deceived in thinking that if we could control the environment we live in, then our lives wouldn't be so terrible. Too often we think that through discipline and determination we can create the life of our dreams.

Yes, some of the things I mentioned in the previous paragraph are good things, but when coupled with a desire for control, they turn bad. The result will ultimately be more worry and anxiety for you, and a lot less control than you think.

Worry is often exhibited in a desire for control. When we worry, our minds are attempting to answer all the questions, go through all the possible outcomes, plan for everything so that we can attain whatever it is that we want.

We want to know it all so that we can control it all!

MORE CONTROL MEANS MORE WORRY

In other words, we want what only God has - unlimited knowledge and control! The problem with control is that the more we have, or the more we think we have, the greater our reason for worry.

Let me give you another example. As missionaries to Ukraine our family travels back to the US once every few years to visit our supporters. This means a lot of travel, and most of it we do by car. I don't really mind driving, but I do have my limits. Thankfully, my wife also drives, so on long trips we take shifts.

When I drive, it's important that I have control of the car because we've got five kids in the back. This year, while driving to a missions conference in Boise, Idaho, we hit a pretty bad snow storm. For about six hours solid, I drove through snow, slush, and ice. For six hours my hands stayed firmly gripped to the steering wheel, eyes on the road, and foot either on the brake or the gas.

Christina didn't feel comfortable driving in the snow, so that meant it was me all the way. By the time we got to our destination, I was exhausted, but it wasn't as much physical exhaustion as it was mental. The brain power it took to be constantly alert, scanning the road ahead, watching out for semis, and being aware of potential dangers drained my mind of resources. All of that was compounded by the fact that I was responsible for the safety of my wife and five children.

When we reached our destination, it felt so great to get out of the car, to rest my eyes and my mind. I was relieved!

Maybe you feel the the same way about your life. Maybe you have felt the strain of trying to control your life for too long. It's time to step out of the car and hand the keys over. Here are a few practical ways you can do that.

HUMBLE YOURSELF

If you want to hand over control to God, you must start by recognizing your own limits and failures. Humility is the first step in releasing control and anxiety.

> *Humble yourselves, therefore, under the*
> *mighty hand of God so that at the proper*
> *time he may exalt you, casting all your anx-*
> *ieties on him, because he cares for you.*
> *(1 Peter 5:6-7)*

At the beginning of 2014, I reviewed the previous year, and as I looked back it was obvious that I had messed up on a lot of things. I shared the following confession on my blog:

I have a confession to make.

I'm not nearly as spiritual, righteous, or holy as you might think. Over the years, I've gotten pretty good at making things look better on the outside than they are on the inside. The reality is that I still struggle with the basic ugly stuff of sin on the inside.

I've had times over the past year when I felt so lazy that I didn't want to bother myself to get up and discipline the kids or help out with the dishes.

There were a few times that I got angry when I should have remained calm, and a few other times when I should have been angry, but instead I remained apathetic.

There were times when my selfishness got the best of me and instead of giving myself in ministry to others, I found excuses so that I could do something for myself.

There were other times when I replied to my family sharply in an unloving way instead of carefully listening and engaging them as a loving father.

Often, instead of turning to God in prayer to help in a difficult circumstance, I simply put myself into the work and tried to figure it out on my own.

Why am I telling you all of this?

Because it's the truth and it's humbling. Looking back is always humbling. It's humbling to see how God worked in us and through us. It's humbling to recognize our failures and realize how God used them for his good. It's humbling to know that we are a small part of God's greater plan.[7]

Did I have a terrible year in 2013? No, not really; in fact, God did a lot in our ministry that year, but it wasn't because I was in control, it was because God was, and that's really the point. We can't relinquish control to God until we realize our own problems, our own inadequacy, and our own sin.

You can choose to be humble now, or wait, and God will eventually humble you; you can choose to give God the control now, or wait, and God will eventually take it from you. I suggest that you not wait!

> *So that at the name of Jesus every knee*
> *should bow, in heaven and on earth and*
> *under the earth, and every tongue confess*
> *that Jesus Christ is Lord, to the glory of*
> *God the Father.*
> *(Philippians 2:10-11)*

EXPAND YOUR UNDERSTANDING

One of the main reasons we fail to give God control is because we fail to understand his abilities. I find that this must be a constant and lifelong pursuit. If you're not regularly exposing yourself to God's goodness, greatness, and glory, you will forget!

---

7 http://sukofamily.org/ugly-truth-about-me/

How do we expand our view of God? Primarily we do this through his Word, the Bible. The Scriptures are full of descriptions of God's power and might. We can see it in many stories, like how God was able to bring his people out of slavery in Egypt, or how he closed the mouths of lions for Daniel, or how Jesus conquered death in the gospels.

When I read the Bible, I often ask myself, "What is this text teaching about who God is?" If you want some good descriptions of God's ability, try reading the following texts.

- Job 38-40
- Isaiah 40
- Revelation 19:11-16

There is another simple way to increase your awe of God and deepen your understanding of his nature and abilities, and that is simply by observing his creation.

David tells us in Psalm nineteen that creation itself speaks of God's glory and greatness.

> *The heavens declare the glory of God, and*
> *the sky above proclaims his handiwork.*
> *Day to day pours out speech, and night to*
> *night reveals knowledge.*
> *There is no speech, nor are there words,*
> *whose voice is not heard.*
> *Their voice goes out through all the earth,*
> *and their words to the end of the world.*
> *In them he has set a tent for the sun, which*
> *comes out like a bridegroom leaving his*
> *chamber, and, like a strong man, runs its*
> *course with joy.*
> *Its rising is from the end of the heavens,*
> *and its circuit to the end of them, and there*
> *is nothing hidden from its heat.*
> *(Psalm 19:1-6)*

Take time to observe the trees, the sky, the magnificence of creation. These all speak of God's awesome power, his amazing abilities, and his beauty. When we observe what he has made, we ought to conscientiously remind ourselves that the same God is at work in our lives, and is able!

Expanding your knowledge of God and your understanding of his greatness will give you all the reason you need to hand over the control of your life to him, and it will strengthen your faith too!

FOCUS ON YOUR RESPONSIBILITIES

I've heard people repeat a common saying that goes like this "Let go and let God." Certainly I appreciate the sentiment, but I think there is also a danger in how we often understand that little saying.

You see, giving over control of your life to God doesn't mean that you get to sit back and relax while God does all the work; it doesn't mean that you have no responsibilities, or that God requires nothing of you.

When you give over control to God, you are simply recognizing the fact that you are unable to control every outcome and you are incapable of determining your destiny. You realize that, ultimately, God has rule over your life, and you willingly subject yourself to his rule.

What we have to understand is that we still have responsibilities, we have to asks that God has called us to do. Instead of trying to ensure that we get exactly what we want, God calls us to simply be faithful in our service to him.

The prophet Samuel exhorted the people of Israel to fear and serve the Lord faithfully.

Only fear the LORD and serve him faith-
fully with all your heart. For consider what
great things he has done for you.
(1 Samuel 12:24)

We can take this advice for ourselves too! Our job is to faithfully serve the Lord, and he is the one who will do great things and provide the results! Rather than working to control the outcome of everything in our life, we need to focus our minds on becoming faithful servants, even in the small things of life!

10

SEEK THE KINGDOM

What do you seek?

Do you seek approval? If you do, then you'll probably struggle with worry about how you look and you'll be constantly thinking about what others might be saying about you.

Do you seek money? Then it's going to be difficult for you not to worry about the economy or losing your job or paying your bills.

Do you seek health? Then you're going worry about eating the wrong thing, getting into a car accident, or getting sick because you didn't wash your hands.

Do you seek another person? Then you're going to worry about that person, and you may worry about how you could go on if you loose that person.

Do you seek a position? Then you're going to worry about whether or not you're working hard enough and doing all the right things on the job. You're going to be more concerned with your resume and your title than you are with doing what's right.

The principle here is simple; your worries tend to follow your highest values and greatest desires in life.

God's solution is simple, change your desires and get rid of your worries!

> *But seek first the kingdom of God and his righteousness, and all these things will be added to you. "Therefore do not be anxious about tomorrow, for tomorrow will be anxious for itself. Sufficient for the day is its own trouble.*
> *(Matthew 6:33-34)*

God's solution is to seek the kingdom of God. In the context of this passage, seeking the Kingdom is contrasted to the most basic things we seek in life. Just two verses earlier Jesus told his disciples,

> *Therefore do not be anxious, saying, 'What shall we eat?' or 'What shall we drink?' or 'What shall we wear?'*
> *(Matthew 6:31)*

If you want to live for any length of time, then food, drink, and clothing aren't nice items to have - they are necessary for your very existence! In Western society, we tend to worry more about getting that promotion or making a fashion statement then we do about having enough food to eat for the next meal!

Jesus brings us back to the most primal needs. If we are not even supposed to worry about the basics, how much more ought we not to worry about the extras in life?

Jesus is not saying that we should not seek to provide for our needs. In fact, there are many other Bible texts that emphasize the importance of working hard and providing for yourself and your family! Paul told Timothy that those who don't provide for their loved ones are worse than unbelievers!

> *But if anyone does not provide for his relatives, and especially for members of his*

> household, he has denied the faith and is
> worse than an unbeliever.
> (1 Timothy 5:8)

The point Jesus is making is that we often elevate our physical and temporary needs far above our spiritual needs! It's an issue of misplaced values and wrong priorities.

We seek satisfaction of the body, thinking that it will also somehow nourish our souls. We spend precious time and energy worrying about how we can fulfill these needs, because we truly believe that if we had a few more dollars saved away we'd be satisfied. We think that if only we had that house with the giant backyard, we would be fulfilled. We presume that the reason we are so unsatisfied is because we are stuck in the wrong job or don't have the funds to purchase that new car.

In the Gospel of Luke, just before Jesus teaches about worry and seeking the kingdom, he gives a great illustration of why this is so important.

> *And he told them a parable, saying, "The*
> *land of a rich man produced plentifully,*
> *and he thought to himself, 'What shall I*
> *do, for I have nowhere to store my crops?'*
> *And he said, 'I will do this: I will tear down*
> *my barns and build larger ones, and there*
> *I will store all my grain and my goods.*
> *And I will say to my soul, "Soul, you have*
> *ample goods laid up for many years; re-*
> *lax, eat, drink, be merry."' But God said to*
> *him, 'Fool! This night your soul is required*
> *of you, and the things you have prepared,*
> *whose will they be?' So is the one who lays*
> *up treasure for himself and is not rich*
> *toward God."*
> *(Luke 12:16-21)*

Was it wrong that this rich man had a plentiful harvest? Absolutely not! Some have mistakenly thought that this parable is about the evils of wealth, but it's not. There are plenty of other places in the Bible where it is obvious that at times God gives wealth to people.

The problem here is in the rich man's misguided desires and misplaced trust. Notice what he says - "Soul, you have ample goods laid up for many years; relax, eat, drink, and be merry."

Honestly, that sounds pretty good, doesn't it? Wouldn't you like to have the confidence that you have a healthy 401k, a nice home in the country that's paid for, and bulging bank account to boot?

TRUST IN STUFF

There are two problems with this situation. The first is that the rich man's trust was in his stuff. He assumed that his big barns filled with grain would save him. He was sure that his wealth was really all he needed. He could proudly say "Relax, eat drink and be merry" because he had provided for himself; by his own hand he had become rich, or so he thought!

This rich man failed to think beyond this life, where his wealth wouldn't do a bit of good. He also failed to acknowledge that God was the true source of his wealth. As a result he trusted in something that was inanimate and temporary instead of someone who is alive and eternal! He believed that this was it; he had arrived, there was no more work for him to do. He was going to enjoy his paradise now because he had earned it!

His faith in his finances let him down big time, they didn't deliver on their promise of "the good life," because that night he died without even having the chance to enjoy his wealth.

God calls this type of person a fool! He's a fool because he put his trust in the wrong thing; he's a fool because he believed the lie that if he could retire early with a nice nest egg, everything would be great!

CONCERN FOR COMFORT

There's a second way the rich man failed, and that has to do with his focus. From this short story, it's obvious that the guy had no concern for spiritual matters. His highest value was himself; just look at how many times he refers to himself!

In this parable, the rich man refers to himself ten times with statements such as: I do; I will; I have; my grain; my barns; my goods; my soul. His primary concern was his own comfort, his greatest goal was to retire, relax, and enjoy life! His main focus was on insuring that he could safely keep everything he earned, as seen in the big barn he built for himself.

Jesus tells us that he laid up "treasure for himself" and he was not "rich towards God." Unfortunately, the rich man was not seeking the kingdom; he was seeking his own treasure and pleasure. It's impossible to seek the kingdom as long as your main goals in life are focused on yourself and on your wealth!

RICH TOWARD GOD

How might this situation have looked if the rich man was rich toward God? I suspect the first thought and first words to come from the rich man, after he realized that the harvest was so great, would be words and thoughts of thanksgiving. He would have understood that his wealth was from the hand of God and he would have acknowledged God for such a blessing.

If the rich man was seeking the kingdom instead of his own treasure, I think he may have next thought of how he could share some of his wealth with those in need and in a way that would promote the righteousness and the values of the kingdom of God. Furthermore, instead of using his great wealth so that he could relax and enjoy life, the person who truly seeks the king-dom would say, "Now that I'm financially taken care of, I can give my life to serving the Lord and serving others!"

When you fail to seek the kingdom, it's like building sandcastles on the beach when the tide is rising. Each wave comes a little closer, and soon enough, they are eating away at the very foun-dation of what you are building. It doesn't matter how fast you repair the damage, eventually your sandcastle will sink back into the shore as the waves wash it away!

The only way to rid yourself of that worry is to focus on some-thing that is lasting, something that won't disappear or wash away, something that is eternal. That's why God's alternative to worry is to seek the Kingdom of God!

Until you replace your anxiety with a deep heart desire for God's Kingdom, you will never truly have victory over it! Until you turn your attention away from your worries and onto the glories of the kingdom of God, you will never really experience the joy of living a worry free life.

Of course it's easy to say that we need to "seek the kingdom" or be "Kingdom minded". It sounds nice and spiritual and most people who have a church background would probably say "amen" if you told them that they just need to focus on the kingdom.

However, when you stop and think about it, there are some real questions here. What exactly did Jesus mean when he said that instead of worrying we should seek the kingdom?

THE KINGDOM IS RIGHTEOUSNESS

The truth is that Jesus didn't just tell us to seek the kingdom, he also tells us to seek righteousness. That's because God's kingdom is a kingdom where righteousness and justice reign supreme. Righteousness means more than doing the right thing; it's about being the right person. Yes, righteousness can be seen in our actions, but notice that Jesus doesn't say "seek first the kingdom and do good things."

Jesus' exhortation is to seek the kingdom and to seek righteousness. In reality, seeking the kingdom is seeking righteousness! All kingdoms gain their character from the king who reigns over them. God is righteous and so is his kingdom. If you seek God you will find his kingdom, and there you will also find righteousness.

But there's a problem - we're not righteous by nature. We do more than just make mistakes; we have evil intentions, we purposefully don't do what we know we should do because we are too lazy, self-centered, or arrogant. Our problem is called "sin," and since we all do it, the Bible calls us sinners and unrighteous.

How can we as sinners seek the kingdom?

THE KINGDOM IS NEW BIRTH

Thankfully, God knew our problem, and he provided a way. Jesus explained this to Nicodemus, one of the religious leaders of Israel, who had come to him secretly late one night with many question.

> *Jesus answered him, "Truly, truly, I say to*
> *you, unless one is born again he cannot see*
> *the kingdom of God."*
> *(John 3:3)*

If you truly want to seek the kingdom of God and be part of the kingdom of God, then, as Jesus said, you need to be born again; you need new life that only Jesus can give you.

How do you do that? Simply by believing Jesus was indeed the Son of God and trusting that his death on the cross and resurrection three days later is sufficient to forgive your sins and give you the righteousness you need to enter the kingdom.

Just a few verses later, Jesus tells Nicodemus:

> *For God so loved the world, that he gave*
> *his only Son, that whoever believes in him*
> *should not perish but have eternal life. For*
> *God did not send his Son into the world to*
> *condemn the world, but in order that the*
> *world might be saved through him. Who-*
> *ever believes in him is not condemned, but*
> *whoever does not believe is condemned*
> *already, because he has not believed in the*
> *name of the only Son of God.*
> *(John 3:16-18)*

If you're ready to start seeking the kingdom of God, the first step you need to take is to believe in Jesus! This simple step will change your life. It will allow the Holy Spirit to change your heart and it will enable you to earnestly seek the kingdom and leave your worries behind!

THE KINGDOM IS PEACE

The apostle Paul also reminds us of Christ's teaching on the kingdom of God in his letter to the church in Rome when he says:

> *For the kingdom of God is not a matter of*
> *eating and drinking but of righteousness*
> *and peace and joy in the Holy Spirit. Who-*
> *ever thus serves Christ is acceptable to God*
> *and approved by men. So then let us pur-*
> *sue what makes for peace and for mutual*
> *upbuilding.*
> *(Romans 14:17-19)*

Pay attention to Paul's instructions here. Those who seek the kingdom do so by pursuing peace and building others up. We seek the kingdom when we pursue kingdom truths in our own life and the lives of others. This includes the truth that Jesus is the only one who can bring true peace to the heart.

Seekers of the kingdom are never self-centered; their lives point to Jesus and they provide a source of help and truth for others!

THE KINGDOM IS NOW

While there is a sense that the kingdom of God has not yet reached it's complete fulfillment, there is also a sense in which the kingdom is now. Jesus explained it like this to a group of religious leaders who were asking him about when the kingdom would come.

> *Being asked by the Pharisees when the*
> *kingdom of God would come, he answered*
> *them, "The kingdom of God is not coming*
> *in ways that can be observed, nor will they*
> *say, 'Look, here it is!' or 'There!' for behold,*
> *the kingdom of God is in the midst of you."*
> *(Luke 17:20-21)*

The Pharisees expected that the Messiah would almost immediately take political control of the nation. Like the rich man, their focus was also off. They believed that if someone could make political changes, that would be enough. Jesus points them to the fact that the kingdom of God begins internally, it begins in the heart.

In that sense, the kingdom of God is already here, because it exists in the hearts and lives of those who willingly have surrendered their wills to the will of God. It exists in the lives of those who have turned their backs on sin and bowed their knee before God in repentance. It exists in the souls of those who willingly choose Jesus as Lord and King of their lives!

In order to kill worry in our lives, we must pay careful attention to our greatest desires, our deepest passions. We must examine what it is that we are reaching for daily and striving towards. Ultimately, if we are looking for fulfillment in this world, we will not find it! What we will find is disappointment and anxiety!

Put aside your desire for wealth, fame, or power. They are all temporary and they will all let you down. Instead, focus on the Kingdom of God. Learn to seek it with your heart and let it grow inside you. Make it your pursuit, because it will never let you down. It is eternal and it holds within it the key to life!

11

DON'T WORRY ABOUT YOUR LOVED ONES

A few years ago, a coworker and I went to visit Peter, a good pastor friend in Ukraine. We had planned to discuss with him some details concerning our Bible Institute, since he was on the school's board of directors.

When we pulled up to the house, his son-in-law greeted us and immediately I sensed that something was wrong. He seemed too serious and quiet. "What's happening?" I asked as he directed us to the house.

"Little Timothy has been missing for most of the day now; all the family is out looking for him," he replied.

His response stopped us momentarily in our tracks. Timothy was Pastor Peter's youngest child, a seven-year-old-boy. There's nothing worse for a parent than not knowing where your child is or what has happened to them. However, for Peter's family it was much worse.

One day about eight years earlier, Peter's youngest daughter didn't come home from school on time. Later that evening the family found her lifeless body beside the railroad tracks. Now that memory and sickening feeling had returned. Timothy had disappeared with no trace.

On top of all of this Peter was battling cancer and because of his poor health, he was unable to leave the house to help the search for his son. How could we discuss business in a situation like this? I was sure that Peter would be in no condition to meet with us.

We entered the house, exchanged greetings, and Peter filled us in on the search for little Timothy. Once he finished, we told him that we understood the situation and we could come back some other time to discuss business. To my surprise Peter looked at us and calmly said, "Why not talk now? The whole family is out looking for Timothy and I have nothing else to do."

A SIMPLE FORMULA

How could he remain calm? How could he focus his attention on something else when his son was missing? The answer is surprisingly simple, yet uncommonly rare to see worked out in real life. Peter's clarity of thought and unworried mind came from the knowledge of two facts. First, he knew that there was nothing else he could do to aid the search for his son. Second, he knew that ultimately God would take care of the situation.

That's it!

It's a simple formula that takes tons of trust to put into action in your life. It's also something that must be practiced on a daily basis. Peter didn't decide to put his trust in God the moment we showed up at the door to meet with him. Peter had been trusting God all along, and that allowed him to continue trusting when he hit a rough patch in life.

So what happened? We had our meeting and later that evening they found Timothy. He had walked to a friend's house and spent the day playing computer games with him!

Many parents struggle with worry over their children. Parents of young children tend to worry about the health and safety of their baby. As the child grows, the worries can change to anxiety over decisions made without the parents input. Parents worry that their child won't know what to do in certain situations, or that he will give into peer pressure and be led astray by his friends.

This type of worry doesn't only happen with our children. We can easily become anxious about a spouse, a sibling, or a good friend. Sometimes we even point to our worry as proof that we really love that person. However, fretting doesn't prove love; on the contrary, it shows a lack of trust and a failure to place our confidence in God.

WORRIED SICK

Take for example Jesus' parents. Of all parents, they had no reason to worry; after all, their son was perfect! But they did worry!

> *When Jesus was twelve years old, they went up to the festival as usual. When the days of the festival were over, they left for home. The young man Jesus stayed behind in Jerusalem, but his parents did not know it. They thought that he was in their group of travelers.*
>
> *After traveling for a day, they started looking for him among their relatives and friends. When they did not find him, they returned to Jerusalem, searching desperately for him.*
>
> *Three days later they found him in the Temple sitting among the teachers, listening to them, and posing questions to them. All who heard him were amazed at his intelligence and his answers. When Jesus' parents saw him, they were shocked.*

*His mother asked him, "Son, why have
you treated us like this? Your father and
I have been worried sick looking for you!"
He asked them, "Why were you looking for
me? Didn't you know that I had to be in my
Father's house?*
(Luke 2:42-49)[8]

Jesus' parents were worried sick for him, yet according to Jesus' answer, they had no need to worry. They should have known that he was in his "Father's house".

I realize the person you are worrying over is not Jesus; however, you can have a confidence that will keep you from being overwhelmed with worry. As Jesus' parents should have known he was in his Father's house, you can also know that your child, spouse, or friend is in the Father's hands.

You are limited by time and space. You can't always be with your child or spouse. There will be times when you do not know where they are or what has happened. However, no matter where they are, you can know that they are not out of God's sight, they are in the Heavenly Father's presence.

THE DECEPTION OF SAFETY

Often we are mistaken in thinking that if we are with our child or loved one, then we can prevent anything bad from happening to them. Unfortunately, this is not always the case.

Recently I went on a day hike with three of my children. For about two hours we hiked up some very steep trail towards the summit of a small peak in the Olympic Mountains. About a quarter of a mile before we reached the peak, we came to a warning sign that read:

---

8 International Standard Version

Caution, maintained trail ends, proceed at your own risk!

However, we could see that some sort of trail continued on after the sign, and we decided to try it out. We would turn around if things looked too dangerous.

As we moved past the sign, the trail opened up along a narrow ridge with a several-hundred-foot-drop-off on each side. The ridge steadily climbed to a point were it met a steep rock face on the left of the trail. Near the bottom of the rock face dangled the end of a rope that someone had tied off above to help hikers traverse that section.

At that point, I thought it wouldn't be wise to let my nine year old daughter continue up the rock face. I decided to help her get back down to the spot where we had passed the warning sign. As we turned around and started heading back down the ridge, I realized that the section of trail we had just climbed seemed a lot more dangerous going down than it had going up!

Suddenly my heart begin to pound and my muscles tensed up. I wasn't worried for myself, I was worried for my daughter. The trail was covered with loose stones and a little slip might not stop until you hit the valley floor hundreds of feet below!

How was I going to get my daughter down safely? What would I do if she slipped? I quickly thought through my options and then I decided to have her go in front of me. I followed closely behind her with a firm grip on her elbow. My thought was that if she slipped I could hopefully keep a good grip on her and prevent her from falling off the edge of the ridge.

However, I also realized that there was a good chance I wouldn't have the strength to hang onto her. My close proximity and my death grip on her elbow didn't guarantee safety!

Honestly, I was surprised by how quickly I became anxious about the situation. I felt helpless! It was at that point that I decided there was one more thing I could do, I could pray! I did pray and it was a simple prayer, "Lord, please keep us safe!"

Times of danger aren't times to impress others with long, deep, theological prayers that utilize archaic vocabulary. Nevertheless, there is a lot of theology packed into that little prayer.

When we ask God for his protection, we recognize that we are limited and God is unlimited, we prove that we can not guarantee safety but God can, we show that we are powerless but he is powerful!

David often speaks of God's protection in the Psalms.

> *Even though I walk through the valley of*
> *the shadow of death, I will fear no evil, for*
> *you are with me; your rod and your staff,*
> *they comfort me.*
> *(Psalm 23:4)*

A simple prayer for safety and protection is exactly what we need to do when we begin to worry about our loved ones. Not only does it call on the only one who can protect them, it gives our minds and hearts something useful to do.

The next time you're tempted to worry about your child, spouse, or friend, remember that wherever they are, they are in God's hand. Use your worry as signal to pray for them and use your prayer to focus your attention on God's abilities to provide safety and protection when you can't!

CHAPTER

12

DON'T WORRY ABOUT YOUR POSSESSIONS

The car you drive, the house you live in, your new tablet, that garage full of unused fitness equipment, and even the clothes on your back, they all have something in common, they can distract you from the most important things in life.

In 1999, my wife and I moved from where we had been attending Bible college in Redding, California, to Tacoma, Washington, where I would be starting seminary in the Fall. We had one car and lived in a small apartment that was part of the school's dormitory for married students. We had only been married for two years and hadn't had the time to accumulate stuff.

My dad came down with his van and a small trailer to help us move. It took a couple of hours to pack up everything we owned and get on our way. Life was simple and our task was clear; study God's Word and prepare for ministry.

As we settled into our new apartment in Tacoma, I began working for a fire and water damage restoration company. The job mainly consisted of cleaning smoke damaged houses and possessions. I found myself dealing with people's stuff every day!

If things weren't too bad, we could go in, do a light cleaning, and be done. However, in the worst cases, we would go in and pack up everything in the house. We would then transport all the contents to our warehouse for cleaning. Depending on the volume of contents it, could take anywhere from several days to several weeks for our crew to get everything cleaned.

It was while working that job that God taught me some very valuable lessons about the potential problems of my own possessions!

THE DIFFERENCE IN ATTITUDES

The first thing I noticed was the difference peoples' attitudes made. Rich, poor, or in-between, it didn't matter how much stuff people had, what mattered was their attitude towards their stuff. I found there is a real world value for all our possessions that is expressed in dollars and cent; then there is the value that we mentally assign to our possessions.

The worth that we give our possessions has nothing to do with it's real world value and everything to do with our attitude. We tend to overvalue our possessions because we also overvalue the worth and purpose in life that we think they give us!

The consequences of overvaluing our possessions can be huge. I noticed that those who placed high worth on their things were devastated by even a small loss. They often appeared bewildered, irritated, anxious, confused, angry, despondent, and physically worn-out. However, those who realized that their possessions held little value were generally more composed and easier to deal with.

THE PURSUIT OF POSSESSIONS

I also learned that the pursuit of possessions can easily consume our space, our time, our money, and even our minds! In extreme cases this is known as hoarding, which is now recognized by many as a mental illness. Hoarders place far greater worth and importance on the items they posses than anyone else does. They find their identity and their self-worth in their possessions. This unhealthy obsession ultimately enslaves them and traps them in their own homes, surrounded by mountains of garbage.

Shortly after I began working for the fire and water damage restoration company, I encountered my first hoarder. From the outside, the house did not appear that out of the ordinary. A smaller 1970's-style rambler in a lower middle-class neighborhood, surrounded by mostly similar homes. The yard was a little overgrown, but besides that, there were really no clues for what lie inside.

As I stepped inside the house, the first thing I noticed was how dark it was. Stacks of boxes blocked most of the windows so that little natural light made it inside the house. The front door opened into the main living area of the house, which consisted of a small kitchen and a living room with a couch, a TV, and a little wood burning stove. Around the outside of the room piles of books and papers left precious wall between them.

Beyond the living room, a door led to the family room, which was the largest room in the house. Instead of finding a spacious area where the family could relax and enjoy time together, I found layers of boxes that had grown from the floor to the ceiling. A narrow trail wound it's way through the walls of boxes.

There were two other rooms in the house that were completely overrun with stuff! One of the bathrooms was so full that we had to open the window from the outside and climb through to gain access!

It took a crew of half a dozen people nearly a week to free the house from its burden of stuff. We discovered that most of the boxes were things purchased from a TV shopping network called QVC and many of them had sat for years unopened!

How did this all happen? The house didn't fill with things overnight. It happened over a number of years. It happened because of the false belief that the purchase of a new item will bring joy and satisfaction. It happened because the owner was deceived and distracted by stuff; stuff that promised fulfillment but only ended up filling her house and entrapping her.

Hoarders give us a powerful example of what happens when we get focused on possessions and allow them to take control of our life. However, you don't have to be a hoarder to practice the same kind of thinking as you go about your daily life.

We make purchases because we think they will be good for us; and they can be, but if we're not careful, our possessions will turn right around and possesses us! The stuff in our life can dictate not only how we spend our time, but what we think about. We end up losing focus on what is really important in this life, our attention moves from the eternal to the temporary, from the spiritual to the material, from the heart of the matter to external issues.

DISTRACTED BY STUFF

In chapter three, we talked about how the word used for worry in the New Testament can literally mean "to distract". Nothing can distract us like our possessions can! This kind of worry does not always include anxiety, but it's just as destructive! In fact, it might even be more dangerous because it can be so deceptive.

We often don't realize how significantly our things influence our life. Before we know it, our new electronics, latest fashions, and helpful gadgets have overwhelmed our space, robbed us of our time, and stolen our attention. We have been consumed by our consumerism, we have traded timeless truths and vital spiritual principles for temporary things and disposable products.

The Bible is not silent on this issue; Jesus himself spoke clearly about the destructive power possessions can have in our life.

As for what was sown among the thorn
bushes, this is the person who hears the
word, but the worries of life and the deceit-
ful pleasures of wealth choke the word so
that it can't produce a crop.
(Matthew 13:22)[9]

When we obtain new things, we tend to think that they are going to make our life easier, but we often fail to remember that the more stuff we have, the more time and energy it requires just to take care of it. Possessions take our energy and our time; they can also steal our attention.

We spend our brain power trying to figure out how to set up our new flat screen TV, or maybe we are thinking of where to put all the new clothes we just bought, or how to organize a garage full of power-tools and sports equipment. Like it or not our things require thought!

The more value we assign to an object, the more likely it is that we will be tempted to worry about it. Just think about it, no one worries about scratching up a twenty-five-year-old car that has 250,000 miles on it! We know that it really won't make a big difference in its value, and most likely it already has a few good scratches and dents in it.

On the other hand, watch how the owner of a brand new car pays attention to where he parks, making sure that he is far from any stray car doors that could chip the paint of his "baby"! The more worth we give to something, the more likely it is that we are going to be worried about what might happen to it.

LIMITING YOUR POSSESSIONS

One simple way to avoid becoming distracted by our possessions is to limit our purchases. Unfortunately, we live in a consum-

---

9 International Standard Version

er-driven society where every commercial, every billboard, and every magazine flaunts its products before our eyes and ears. They promise to make our lives more exciting and fulfilling. Movie stars and top models gush with praise as they tout the miraculous qualities of the items which they are being paid to push.

The end result is that we often think that we can't live without these things that we've somehow managed to live without our entire lives! Before we follow the herd to local shopping malls and online dealers to make our purchases here are a couple of things to contemplate.

SEVEN THINGS TO CONSIDER BEFORE MAKING A PURCHASE

1. New things tend to wear out faster than things that were built years ago.
2. New things cost more. (If you really need something see if you can get it secondhand first.)
3. It can be cheaper to fix the old than buy a new one!
4. There are often hidden costs for new purchases. (If you buy a new laptop, then you might also want to buy a case, a mouse, etc...)
5. New things only make you feel better for a short time.
6. New things can be wasteful. (They waste money, time, space, packaging.)
7. New things make us want more new things. (It doesn't take long before the new thing isn't new.)

NINE ALTERNATIVES TO MAKING NEW PURCHASES

1. Fix something broken and make it new again.
2. Re-purpose an old or unused item you have laying around your house.
3. Invite a neighbor over for tea.
4. Make a phone call or even a trip to see friends far away.
5. Write a handwritten note.

6. Play with your kids.
7. Have a cup of coffee with your spouse.
8. Make a donation to your church, to a missionary, or any other non-profit.
9. Volunteer to serve in a ministry.

13

DON'T WORRY ABOUT YOUR IMAGE

Growing up, Sunday afternoons were always filled with guests; some of them invited and some of them just showed up. But it wasn't only on Sundays, we had people in our house a lot! It was a rare day when we didn't have someone visiting us, dropping by for coffee, or showing up for dinner!

The fact that my mother had eight children to take care of didn't stop her from having guests in the home. It was so common that I didn't even give it a second thought, at least not until I started having kids. With a family of my own, I suddenly realized the work and sacrifice it takes, and the mindset that goes along with it!

I noticed that there's a big difference between being hospitable and entertaining guests. My mother didn't entertain guests. Yes, she would feed them and even put them up for a night or two, or a few months! But she didn't entertain them!

The difference between entertaining and being hospitable may sound trivial, but it represents an approach and a way of thinking that are polar opposites. Take the example of Mary and Martha and the differences in their approach to having Jesus as a guest in their home.

> *But Martha was distracted with much*
> *serving. And she went up to him and said,*
> *"Lord, do you not care that my sister has*
> *left me to serve alone? Tell her then to help*
> *me." But the Lord answered her, "Martha,*
> *Martha, you are anxious and troubled*
> *about many things, but one thing is nec-*
> *essary. Mary has chosen the good portion,*
> *which will not be taken away from her.*
> *(Luke 10:40-42)*

How would you react if you found out that Jesus was coming to your house for dinner? This is the same guy who earlier fed 5,000 people with five loaves of bread and two fish, and now he's going to eat the bread you made!

- What will he think of your home?
- Will it be clean enough?
- Will he be impressed with your culinary abilities?
- Will he ask for seconds?
- Will he even notice that you repainted the dinning room walls to match the table cloth?
- Will he comment on your fine china?
- Will he praise you for your well-decorated home?

Imagine Martha's shock when she found out that Jesus did not appreciate all she was doing for him! Not only did he not appreciate it, but he effectively scolded her, not because of what she had done, but because of how she was thinking and the choices that her thinking led her to make!

Jesus told her, "You are anxious and troubled by many things." Jesus didn't scold Martha for being hospitable, he scolded her for being distracted and anxious. He scolded her for not paying attention to the most important aspect of having a guest in your home, which is simply spending time with them, conversing with them, and listening to them.

Unfortunately, Martha's focus was on entertainment, not hospitality. Martha was more concerned about whether or not the floors were swept, the roast was well seasoned, and the place settings were perfect than she was with spending time with Jesus.

Ultimately, she wasn't doing these things for Jesus, she was doing them for herself, and that's the difference between true hospitality and entertaining guests!

Martha was consumed with the preparations because she wanted everything to be perfect. As odd as it sounds, I think that she may have had a desire to impress Jesus with her effort. She wanted Jesus to think, "Wow, Martha is an amazing hostess, I've never been treated this well before!"

Martha was concerned with her image; she figured that if she entertained Jesus better than others, then he would love her and praise her over others. This wrong focus kept her from doing the one thing she needed to do more than anything else, which was to sit at Jesus' feet and listen to his words of truth.

The one thing I remember from my mother's hospitality was that it was always simple and never lavish! Yes, we would tidy up the house if we knew guests were coming, but we wouldn't pull out any special china. The meal could be as simple as tuna fish sandwiches on paper plates, and no one complained because there was always plenty of time to enjoy each other's company and relax in each other's presence.

It's impossible to be hospitable when you're focused on what others might think of you. This is an easy trap to fall into and it will always lead to anxiety and worry! In my experience, those who are worried about their image tend to have few (if any) guests in their home. It becomes too difficult for them to makes sure the home is properly cleaned and all the preparations are done to perfection. Their concern with what people will think builds a barrier between them and others and keeps them from building healthy relationships.

The same principles that apply to hospitality, and can be seen in the lives of Martha and Mary, also apply to many other areas of life. We live in a world that is dominated by a focus on the outward appearance. Excessive attention to clothing, make-up, and body appearance results in anxiety over image.

There is even a condition called Body Dysmorphic Disorder (BDD). People who have BDD focus so much on their body's appearance that they become obsessed with perceived imperfections. This obsession leads to anxiety and uncontrollable compulsive behavior.

What are some of the signs of BDD? According to The Anxiety and Depression Association of America, they are the following:

- Camouflaging (with body position, clothing, makeup, hair, hats, etc.)
- Comparing body part to others' appearance
- Seeking surgery
- Checking in a mirror
- Avoiding mirrors
- Skin picking
- Excessive grooming
- Excessive exercise[10]

Once again, it's easy to see how anxiety can be destructive! BDD may be an extreme case but let's think about how worry over image can affect other areas of life.

CHILD-RAISING

Often parents become more worried about their childrens' behavior in public than they are at home. Why? Because they know that their childrens' behavior reflects on their parenting skills and their image.

In order to promote their image in public, they may bribe their

10 http://www.adaa.org/understanding-anxiety/related-illnesses/other-related-conditions/body-dysmorphic-disorder-bdd

children, and when that doesn't work, it can lead to anger and frustration in the parent. This frustration is often later taken out on the child who doesn't understand why their parents have a different standard in public than at home.

PURCHASES

Whether it's a new car, a new dress, or new home, we often put great significance into how others might think of us based upon our purchases. In order to impress others and bolster our image, we can easily get ourselves into debt and make purchases that we don't need and maybe don't even want!

RELATIONSHIPS

There is status in who you know and who you are seen with. Become too worried about your image, and you'll find yourself avoiding interaction with people who you think might be bad for your image and pursuing relationships with those that will "help" your image.

Remember that Jesus was called a friend of tax-collectors and sinners. He wasn't worried about his image and he even got in trouble by those who thought he associated too much with un-desirable people.

As Jesus passed on from there, he saw
a man called Matthew sitting at the tax
booth, and he said to him, "Follow me."
And he rose and followed him. And as Jesus
reclined at table in the house, behold, many
tax collectors and sinners came and were
reclining with Jesus and his disciples.
(Matthew 9:9-10)

MINISTRY

Worry over ministry image can be a particularly deceptive and dangerous pitfall for those who serve in a ministry context. We'd like to think that our ministry is selfless and done only for the glory of God, but often that isn't the case.

If we're not careful, we can easily begin to groom our ministry in a way that will evoke the praise and admiration of others. That's exactly what Jesus was talking about when he warned his disciples about practicing their righteousness before others.

Beware of practicing your righteousness before other people in order to be seen by them, for then you will have no reward from your Father who is in heaven.

Thus, when you give to the needy, sound no trumpet before you, as the hypocrites do in the synagogues and in the streets, that they may be praised by others. Truly, I say to you, they have received their reward.

But when you give to the needy, do not let your left hand know what your right hand is doing, so that your giving may be in secret. And your Father who sees in secret will reward you. And when you pray, you must not be like the hypocrites.

For they love to stand and pray in the synagogues and at the street corners, that they may be seen by others. Truly, I say to you, they have received their reward. (Matthew 6:1-5)

The Pharisee's main motivation in giving to the poor was to receive praise and admiration from the people. It even appears that they designed their ministry for more publicity, to make sure that everyone was aware of their great acts of generosity, or heard their deep theological prayers.

It's easy to condemn the Pharisees for their obvious hypocritical and self-centered approach to ministry; however, it's also easy to fall into the same trap.

One of the greatest signs that you have become too concerned about your image in ministry is worry. Do you find yourself often thinking about how others will react, what they will say, and what they will think of you? If you do, then it's time to make a change and get your focus off yourself and onto God!

HOW TO GET OVER YOUR IMAGE PROBLEM

It turns out that worry over your image is really nothing more than simple pride! That means it's a sin. It happens when you get your focus off the things that truly matter. It happens when you place a higher value on what others think about you than what God knows about you!

In reality, others are probably not thinking about you nearly as much as you think they're thinking about you! It's even a bit arrogant to assume that those around you spend that much time thinking about you.

In order to get out of the image trap, we must change our thinking and we must change our values. As long as we place a high value on our status, appearance, and prestige, then worry over our image will continue to rule our life and our thinking.

Let me say this as clearly as possible, stop thinking so much of yourself! That's where you need to start!

Were you unable to clean every nook and cranny of your home

before guests showed up? That's OK! They didn't come to inspect your floors; they came to spend time with you!

Did your kids misbehave in public? Guess what, you're not the only one! Don't worry about what other parents think of you, but rather, focus on training your child consistently in a way that will give him or her a strong faith and a great foundation for life.

As we learn to think less of ourselves in these potentially image-destroying situations, it makes it increasingly simpler and easier to focus our attention on those issues that really do matter. We need to stop asking and stop caring so much about what others think about us, and instead look at what God values and what he knows about us!

> But the LORD said to Samuel, "Do not look
> on his appearance or on the height of his
> stature, because I have rejected him. For
> the LORD sees not as man sees: man looks
> on the outward appearance, but the LORD
> looks on the heart.
> (1 Samuel 16:7)

God lays it out here for Samuel; he's not concerned with brawns and beauty! God looks at something only he can see clearly, and that's the heart!

What does that mean for our image? That means we need to be much more concerned with being who God wants us to be on the inside, rather than acting in a way to get the approval of others on the outside.

It means faithfulness over fashion, principles over popularity, and integrity over image! Ultimately, it means honoring God with who we are rather than honoring ourselves by catering to the opinions of others.

The prophet Micah puts it well when he says,

*He has told you, O man, what is good; and
what does the LORD require of you but to
do justice, and to love kindness, and to walk
humbly with your God?*
(Micah 6:8)

When we become more concerned with what the Lord requires rather than what man thinks, our image worries will vanish!

14

DON'T WORRY ABOUT YOUR FINANCES

When my wife and I got married, I didn't have a regular job and she couldn't legally work in the US. Christina had come to the States to study at Bible college on a student visa, which didn't allow for employment. We knew it would take a few months to get the paperwork done.

We only had a few dollars in our pockets when we decided to get married. You might think that we just put everything on our credit card, but we didn't because we didn't have one.

I wore an old tuxedo that I had bought when I sang in choir in high school. A friend let Christina borrow her wedding dress. A lady in church volunteered to do the flowers, and another woman said she would do the cake. For food we basically did a potluck that was organized by our church. An uncle took pictures and my brother did video.

Our main expense was renting the church facility which cost us around $400. Thankfully, we were able to pay for that from the wedding gifts!

Shortly after we married, we headed down to Redding, California, to start our second year of Bible college. We arrived with almost nothing. I had earned a little bit of money doing odd jobs over the summer, but it wasn't going to be enough to pay for school and put food on the table too!

A friend sold me his 1979 Chevy Chevette for $300, so we at least had economical transportation. Christina began working in the college library for five dollars an hour, but that money went only to decrease our school bill. Most of that year I struggled to find regular work. I picked up a paper route for a couple hundred bucks a month and when they had work, I'd spend my afternoons cleaning for a fire and water damage restoration company. On Sundays I would often preach in churches in the surrounding areas that didn't have pastors; they would usually give me a honorarium; for which we were very grateful!

That year we learned to trust God for everything. There were no guarantees that we would be able to pay our rent on time, but we always did. On several occasions funds, would miraculously show up in an unmarked envelope in our mail box!

We realized that God was taking care of us and we began keeping a journal of all the ways that he provided. Often it was the little things, like someone inviting us over for dinner and sharing a meal with us, which meant that we would spend less in groceries that week. Our budget for food was $30 a month, and while we didn't always meet our budget, we were often pretty close.

To tell you the truth, we didn't have much and we also didn't worry much. It was clear that God was providing! Having little meant life was simple and as long as we could get through another day we were content.

Nothing can kill your contentment and joy quicker than financial worries. What can keep you from worrying about money? Often we make the mistake of thinking that if we had more money then we could pay our bills and the worrying would stop. This is not necessarily the case.

There are three categories when it comes to financial fretting. There are those who worry about having money to pay for their basic needs, those who worry about how to pay for what they have already purchased, and those who worry about how to keep what they have already paid for.

THE POOR

Those who worry about having enough money to pay for their basic needs are the poor. It's easy to think that you're poor but most likely you're not. If you purchased this book, then it's quite unlikely that you are truly poor. When the Bible talks about the poor, it's not referring to the approximately 50 million Americans who live under the poverty line!

Poverty in Bible times was not having the means to pay for your next meal or any of the other basic needs in life. The Bible often speaks of God's care for the poor; just read Psalm 72! One of Jesus' main purposes in coming was to preach the gospel to the poor (Luke 4:18). Jesus also preached about the poor (Luke 21:1-4) and churches were encouraged to give to the poor (Romans 15:25-26).

The poor are not forgotten in the Bible and they are not forgotten by God. Ironically, financial worries are often a much bigger problem with those of us who would not be considered poor by Biblical standards.

The remaining two categories of money worriers are debtors and misers. Those who worry about how to pay for what they've purchased are called debtors and those who worry about keeping the money and things they have already acquired are called misers; both are equally destructive.

Debtors and misers share some surprising traits! Both are consumed with an unhealthy fixation on finances, both are often willing to compromise their morals if it will help them attain their financial desires, and neither are very generous!

MISERS

How do you know if you're a miser? A miser is someone who, despite the fact that he has enough or more than enough to live on, is constantly looking for ways to economize and to insure his wealth.

One great example is J. Paul Getty who was the worlds richest man until his death in 1976. Despite his billionaire status, he is well known for being a miser. He was so concerned with saving money that he had a coin operated phone installed in his home for guests, so that they wouldn't run up his phone bill![11]

Now I doubt that many who are reading this book are billionaires and I'm almost certain that you don't have a coin operated phone in your home. However, we can easily be misers in the smaller things. A miser is anyone who places their wealth above other more important values like relationships, kindness, and faithfulness.

The writer of Proverbs describes it like this,

Do not eat the bread of a man who is stingy; do not desire his delicacies, for he is like one who is inwardly calculating. "Eat and drink!" he says to you, but his heart is not with you. You will vomit up the morsels that you have eaten, and waste your pleasant words.
(Proverbs 23:6-8)

Is it difficult for you to give up your things? Do you find that you are always analyzing the bottom line, trying to earn more, spend less, and safeguard your wealth? Are you more interested in how your stocks are doing when you wake up than you are with opening your Bible and spending some time with God? Do you find yourself looking down on those who are less prosperous than you?

---

11 Getty, 1976, pg.319

If you answered "yes" to any of those questions then you may be a miser.

Jesus gives a warning to misers, he says,

> *Do not lay up for yourselves treasures on earth, where moth and rust destroy and where thieves break in and steal, but lay up for yourselves treasures in heaven, where neither moth nor rust destroys and where thieves do not break in and steal. For where your treasure is, there your heart will be also.*
> *(Matthew 6:19-21)*

> *No one can serve two masters, for either he will hate the one and love the other, or he will be devoted to the one and despise the other. You cannot serve God and money.*
> *(Matthew 6:24)*

Here are the facts, money is a cruel master who, if allowed, will enslave you and make you work for temporary treasures! There's only one way to freedom and that's a change of heart.

Misers need to understand that all wealth is temporary; it can be gone tomorrow! Yes, it's important to use wise biblical principles that include saving some money, but we should not put our hope in money nor give all our attention to it.

A heart that serves God as its master sees money in a completely different light. Money is not a tool to get what I want, money is not something I deserve, money will not bring me joy, rather, money is a resource to be used for God's glory! Whether we have little or much, our contentment comes not from a growing bank account, but from God, who provides far beyond the things dollars and cents can purchase!

DEBTORS

Those who have fallen into debt also need to gain a proper understanding if they want to avoid worry.

Debt doesn't just drain your bank account; if you're not careful, it can suffocate your spiritual life too! When unpaid bills are piling up on the desk, it's easy for your focus to get off of God. Worry that more collection notices will arrive can plague you, and the mental effort it takes to figure a way out from under a mountain of debt can leave you exhausted.

Don't be deceived, paying off your debts won't always relieve you of your money worries. Yes, more money may help you pay your bills, but your worry over finances may lie deeper, at the heart level.

If you don't correctly understand what caused you to go into debt it's very likely that you will find yourself in that place again. More often than not, financial worries are brought on by unwise choices not inevitable circumstances.

Yes, there is the unexpected loss of a job or hospital bills that can catapult an otherwise financially stable person into debt, but let's be honest, most of the time it's not one big thing, but a lot of little things that lead us into debt.

It's impulse purchases of stuff that you really, really want, but don't necessarily need, it's living without a budget, or not sticking to a budget, it's using credit cards instead of cash because you don't want to wait another month!

Consumer debt is often a combination of greed, impatience, and unwise choices. Take the advice of Proverbs.

Wealth gained hastily will dwindle,
but whoever gathers little by little will
increase it.
(Proverbs 13:11)

> *A slack hand causes poverty, but the hand*
> *of the diligent makes rich. He who gath-*
> *ers in summer is a prudent son, but he*
> *who sleeps in harvest is a son who brings*
> *shame. (Pro 10:4-5)*

If you're worried about your debt, here are a ten things that you need to start doing right now!

1. Evaluate your reason for getting into debt.
2. Create and live by a budget.
3. Sell anything you don't need or is costing you extra money to maintain.
4. Start paying down your debt every month.
5. Start putting something aside every month, no matter how small.
6. Learn to understand the difference between wants and needs.
7. Work hard.
8. Don't try to "get rich quick."
9. Be thankful for all you have.
10. Trust God to provide.

Your debt may or may not be the result of unwise choices, but no matter how you got into debt, worry over your debt is a sin and it's something you can change right now. Jesus clearly teaches us that God can and will provide for our needs!

> *Therefore I tell you, do not be anxious*
> *about your life, what you will eat or what*
> *you will drink, nor about your body, what*
> *you will put on. Is not life more than food,*
> *and the body more than clothing?*

> *Consider the lilies of the field, how they*
> *grow: they neither toil nor spin, yet I tell*
> *you, even Solomon in all his glory was not*
> *arrayed like one of these. But if God so*
> *clothes the grass of the field, which today is*

alive and tomorrow is thrown into the oven,
will he not much more clothe you, O you
of little faith? Therefore do not be anxious,
saying, 'What shall we eat?' or 'What shall
we drink?' or 'What shall we wear?'
(Matthew 6:25, 28-31)

The logic here is simple; first, we must recognize that there are things in life more important than food and clothing (or money). Second, we must understand that we are valuable to God and he can and will provide. Third, we need to realize that worry will never put food on the table or pay the rent!

According to Jesus, this all points back to our faith! Jesus isn't saying that the stronger your faith is, the better God will provide for you; rather he's saying that God is providing for you, and if you only believed that, you wouldn't be so worried!

This is a truth that we must remind ourselves of often! My friend Tom put it this way.

> ...it's important to remind myself daily, that each day is placed before me by His Grace, and I should walk that path by faith, knowing that the sufficiency for that day is provided by Christ. If I take my eyes off Christ (seems like even for a moment) I begin to think about how life would be easier if I had more of this or that. All I ever need is found in the fact that I am "in Him," and that should be my motivation. That's when I have no financial stress, because that's when I cease to create the reasons to be stressed.
> — Tom Wilhelmson

Whether you are poor, a debtor, or a miser, your goal should be to get your focus onto God! Place your faith firmly in him and he will provide for your needs and give you peace of mind in all your financial dealings.

DON'T WORRY ABOUT YOUR HEALTH AND SAFETY

For my birthday one year, my father-in-law purchased me the gift of a ride in an ultra-light. Now you have to keep in mind that this was in the mid 1990's on a beach along the Dnieper river in Cherkassy, Ukraine. The guy who flew the ultralight pulled it behind an old Soviet Lada. He and a couple of friends just happened to show up on the beach an hour earlier and we watched as they got the ultralight ready to fly and took it for a few test runs.

That's when my father-in-law got the idea of asking if he could purchase a ride for me. For about five dollars the owner agreed to give me a short flight. This flying machine was made of aluminium tubes over which the canvas wings were stretched. The cockpit, if you can call it that, was two canvas seats hung between the aluminium tubing. Directly behind the seats was the motor and the propeller.

The cockpit was completely open to the air, which meant the only thing to hold me in was the seat-belt. I climbed in and began to fiddle with the seat-belt. The pilot looked at me through his aviator goggles and simply said, "Ne nada!" which means "You don't need that!"

To this day I'm not sure why I did it, but against my better judgement I let the seat-belt dangle from the sides of that canvas seat as the motor roared to life. Within a few seconds we were accelerating down the beach. I had a video camera in one hand and the other hand had a death grip on the aluminium tube that ran along side my seat.

The higher we climbed, the more I began to think, "Why didn't I put my seat-belt on?" And then, "What will happen if a gust of wind throws us sideways?" The hand that was holding on for dear life began to ache a bit as we went into a sharp turn and I squeezed even harder. Thankfully, it was a short flight and after a few turns we started to descend. The approaching ground gave me hope, and as we touched down, I exhaled and my grip loosened. I had made it!

I've flown much higher before. I've flown much further. I've flown much faster. I've been on planes that flew through thunder storms with lightening hitting the wings. I've been on planes that had to turn around because of mechanical problems. Yet, I've never been so worried and scared as I was during those few minutes aloft in an ultralight over the Dnieper River.

What was the difference between my ride in the ultralight and all my other flights?

In one word it was — TRUST!

You see, I didn't have a lot of reason to trust this pilot that just showed up on the beach while we were celebrating my birthday. I didn't know him and I didn't know what kind of flight experience he had. I wasn't sure how well he kept up his ultralight, but I did know for sure that the FAA hadn't approved it!

When I fly on a commercial plane, I assume that their pilots meet strict standards, have hundreds of hours of experience, and are guided by FAA rules. I also assume that the airlines keep good care of their planes, that they have qualified mechanics who make sure that everything works properly, and that they test them regularly for defects. I also know that there are seat-belts, life vests, life rafts, and other safety equipment on board.

All of these things serve to give me confidence that even if we are flying through a thunderstorm, the pilot knows what he's doing and is equipped to fly his plane safely. That is to say, I have more trust in a well-trained pilot, flying a well-maintained airplane for an airline who has a good safety record, than I do for a pilot who just showed up on the beach one day!

A TRUST ISSUE

In reality, all worry over your health and safety is a trust issue. If you're not trusting God as your pilot, then you will struggle with fears over your well-being and possibly over the well-being of those you love.

There are only two ways to get over this type of anxiety; the first is to try and convince yourself that you are safe and that you will never get sick or be injured. Some people succeed in doing this, but their success is temporary. The truth is that you will get sick, you will have health problems, and eventually those health problems will kill you!

I'm not trying to be morbid, but I am trying to help you realize that in this life there is no such thing as ultimate safety; no one avoids all sickness and no one avoids death. Whether you die in a plane crash or your heart simply stops beating as you sleep, death will come as a result of some sort of physical problem.

We need to get it out of our minds that we can avoid all physical pain and problems by washing our hands, exercising, and eating the right foods. Don't misunderstand me, you should do what you can to stay healthy and safe, but don't think that if you do everything right you will not experience any physical problems.

We live in a world that is under the curse of sin. Since the day that Adam and Eve disobeyed God, we live in a dying world. I know that doesn't give you a lot of hope, but I told you that there are two ways to get over anxiety about your health and physical well-being.

The first way, as I mentioned, is to deny that you will have any problems, just to put it out of your mind. That's no good because it's not true! You will encounter health problems.

ULTIMATE SAFETY

The second method, and the only one that really works, is to put your trust in God who created your body. He is the only one who has the ability to provide you with ultimate safety!

David is a great example of someone who should have been very worried about his safety, but he wasn't! Early on we see him taking on Goliath when everyone else was afraid to fight him. King Saul looked at David and said,

> *You are not able to go against this Phi-*
> *listine to fight with him, for you are*
> *but a youth, and he has been a man of*
> *war from his youth.*
> *(1 Samuel 17:33)*

Saul was comparing David's physical stature and experience with Goliath's and it was no match. However, Saul forgot one important aspect, David trusted in the Lord!

David's response is simple and clear.

> *The LORD who delivered me from the paw*
> *of the lion and from the paw of the bear will*
> *deliver me from the hand of this Philistine.*
> *(1 Samuel 17:37)*

David knew the situation was dangerous. David knew Goliath was taller, stronger, and a more skilled fighter than he was. David also knew something that the others didn't; he knew that God had the ability to keep him safe no matter the circumstances.

Personal experience combined with Biblical truth gave David the solid confidence he needed to face Goliath without worrying about the outcome! David's complete trust in the Lord to keep him safe comes out in many of the Psalms he wrote.

In peace I will both lie down and sleep; for you alone, O LORD, make me dwell in safety.
(Psalm 4:8)

Even though I walk through the valley of the shadow of death, I will fear no evil, for you are with me; your rod and your staff, they comfort me.
(Psalm 23:4)

A Song of Ascents. I lift up my eyes to the hills. From where does my help come? My help comes from the LORD, who made heaven and earth. He will not let your foot be moved; he who keeps you will not slumber. Behold, he who keeps Israel will neither slumber nor sleep. The LORD is your keeper; the LORD is your shade on your right hand. The sun shall not strike you by day, nor the moon by night. The LORD will keep you from all evil; he will keep your life. The LORD will keep your going out and your coming in from this time forth and forevermore.
(Psalm 121)

These are good reminders that ultimately only God has the ability to keep us from physical harm. We need to trust him with our very lives every day! Of course, that doesn't mean we should begin living recklessly, driving without our seat-belt on, or disregarding common sense health practices. God calls us to live wisely and to make healthy and safe choices in life.

David had many reasons to worry about his safety, there were lions and bears who threatened him while he was a shepherd boy, then there was Goliath, but worse than these was King Saul. As David grew in popularity, Saul became jealous and he made it his life's goal to capture and kill David.

A CONFIDENCE THAT CAN'T BE SHAKEN

Imagine if you lived in a country where the president's main goal was to kill you! That would give you all kinds of reasons to worry! Yet, we find that David didn't just avoid worry, he slept in peace, (Psalm 4:8) and he had a glad heart (Psalm 16:9)!

> I have set the LORD always before me; because he is at my right hand, I shall not be shaken. Therefore my heart is glad, and my whole being rejoices; my flesh also dwells secure. (Psalm 16:8-9)

Notice David's words here, "I have set the LORD always before me." The secret to David's confidence was that he saw God in every situation. He realized that God was with him, he knew that God was leading him through every circumstance, and he believed that God really was in control.

When we begin to see God at work in every day life, it becomes increasingly difficult to worry! The problem is that we often don't have the Lord set before us. Instead, we set potential problems before us and our brains run amuck frantically trying to avoid any possibility of harm. We forget that God is with us and we fail to realize that he is involved in everything we do!

It's impossible to avoid all danger and it's not wise to ignore it either. We can, however, face that danger head on with God at our side! That's what David did and look at how it affected his life.

As a result of putting the Lord always before him, David tells us that he will not be shaken. Despite the fact that someone was out to kill him, David was not panic-stricken, rattled, or fearful! Instead, he was firmly rooted in the assurance that only the Lord could give him.

With his confidence solidly fixed on God, David was not given to doubts, fear, or alarm. He moved forward with purpose and clarity. Because his mind was focused on God's abilities rather than theoretical dangers, his thinking was not overcome by anxiety or distracted by worry.

However, David did more than simply avoiding worry. He tells us that his heart is glad and his whole being rejoices. What a contrast! Wouldn't you love to be glad and have joy instead of fretting over your health? When you put your confidence in God's abilities, you can experience joy in the face of danger!

LIFE BEYOND THE GRAVE

Certainly God is able to keep you safe in every situation, but that doesn't mean that he always does. Sometimes God allows you to get sick, become injured, and eventual, God will allow you to die! David knew and understood this well. We find that David's confidence in God extended beyond the grave and into eternity!

David says,

> *For you will not abandon my soul to Sheol,*
> *or let your holy one see corruption.*
> *(Psalm 16:10)*

Often commentators point out that this is a prophetic statement referring to Jesus Christ, who after he was crucified was resurrected on the third day. Certainly, this text does point to Jesus, but David was also talking about his own body here.

David's hope transcended this life. He knew that even if his enemy did kill him, it wouldn't be the end. God's resurrection power could even overcome death! When we understand this awesome power, it kills our worries over health and safety! It allows us to move forward in our life. It allows us to take risks for the sake of righteousness! It gives us peace of mind and hope for the future!

CHAPTER

MAKE DECISIONS SIMPLE

Worry can often make decisions a grueling and time-consuming process. In chapter five I talked about the problem of asking "what if..." and how that can be a never-ending question; one that we cannot fully answer because we are not God. Nevertheless, we all have to make decisions from time to time, and if you're easily given to worry, even the smallest decision can be tough to navigate.

Every decision we make brings with it a set of theoretical outcomes. This is what we often worry about. We want to make the best decision, the safest decision, the decision that will be most profitable, most comfortable, and provide the least amount of risk.

Is there a way to simplify the decision-making process? Is there a way to confidently determine the best course and move on? I believe there is. In this chapter I want to share with you a few tips on how to streamline your decisions and clarify your choices. In order to do this, we must begin by asking ourselves several questions.

QUESTION 1

IS IT A MORAL ISSUE?

This may seem over-simplified, but it's a vital step and it should always be the first question before making a significant decision. Too often we get caught up in the moment or in the emotion of what's happening and we fail to address this basic question.

Another way to look at this question is like this; would it violate a Biblical command to say "yes" to this decision or would it violate a Biblical command to say "no" to this decision?

It's easy to worry about making sure you are doing God's will in your life. You may feel that in the past you missed an opportunity or made a poor decision about what job to take or what house to buy or what school to go to. You fear that you missed God's will, and as a result, you missed out on the best God has for you.

On the other hand, you may be tempted to spend days and months worrying about the future and wondering how to determine whether or not God wants you to pursue this degree or that degree, whether or not you should move to a different area of the country or start a new business or have more children, and the list goes on.

It would be nice to open God's Word and flip to the chapter called "Life Plan," and there you could read the detailed personal plan God has for your life. We wish that God could just tell us what decisions we should make. It seems like it would make life so much easier!

In many situations God isn't as concerned about the exact decisions you make as he is about the type of decisions you make. We tend to get caught up in thinking only about the practical outcomes of our decision. That means when we are looking to find a new job, we tend to make that decision based on how much the job will pay, where it is located, and how much work they will require of us.

126

When we are looking to buy a house, we are mainly concerned with how much it will cost and how big the yard will be and how nice the neighborhood is. Now, don't misunderstand me, those things may all be important, but they are not the most important!

God wants us to make moral decisions. He wants us to follow Biblical standards. He doesn't just want us to get a good job or a bigger house or a beautiful spouse, he wants us to pursue a job that wouldn't cause us to compromise our beliefs, purchase a home that wouldn't serve our own pride, and find a spouse who is committed to pursuing righteousness with us!

God wants us to make the type of decisions that are righteous, ethical, and honorable. Therefore, before you make any decision, you must simply ask yourself if there are any moral issues involved.

Will making this decision involve any of the following?

- Dishonesty
- Immorality
- Lust
- Greed
- Pride
- Selfishness
- Laziness
- Bitterness
- Law-breaking
- Etc...

If any of the above are involved, then your decision is easy! Don't do it! There will also be times when your inaction will produce immoral results, and thus the reverse is also true. If not making that decision involves any of the above, then you need to step forward in faith and do the right thing.

Here's why I love this question - if it is morally wrong to do whatever it is that you're thinking of doing, then that's it! You're decision making is done. You don't have to look any further, you don't have worry about it any more because the choice is clear.

QUESTION 2

IS IT A WISDOM PRINCIPLE?

Many of the decisions we must make on a daily basis aren't primarily moral issues. For instance, when I get up in the morning I decide if I want to eat cold cereal or hot oatmeal for breakfast, then I decide if I'm going to wear the striped polo shirt or the solid button-up shirt. Before I go out the door I might need to decide between sneakers or dress shoes.

Generally, these types of decisions don't have to deal with moral issues. It's not immoral to choose oatmeal over cereal or sneakers over dress shoes. This can also be the case with many larger decisions in life. For instance, there's no direct Biblical command that would make you choose a career as a medical doctor over a career as an airline pilot. If you're shopping for a home, you won't find a Scripture verse that tells you that if you want to obey God then you should buy the house on 12th street instead of the house on 13th street. While there are no moral issues at the root of these types of decisions, there are Biblical principles given in God's Word to help us.

Biblical principles of wisdom help us discern between what often appears to be two options where neither is "sinful" or "wrong." Yet, there could still be significant ramifications as a result of making that decision.

Here's a simple example: I like to drink coffee and I don't think drinking coffee is sinful. In the morning I just love to pour myself a cup and slowly sip it while I study God's Word. It helps my body wake up and my mind to be alert as I contemplate the passage at hand. I consider drinking coffee in the morning a wise and pleasant thing to do.

However, if I were to do the same thing at night right before bed, that would not be so wise. Drinking coffee at night tends to make me stay awake, which means I will be much more tired if I want to wake up at the same time in the morning. Is it a sin to drink coffee after nine PM? Probably not, but it certainly isn't wise!

The Bible emphasizes the importance of using wisdom in daily living so much, that it devotes the entire book of Proverbs to the pursuit of wisdom!

> *Get wisdom; get insight; do not forget,*
> *and do not turn away from the words of*
> *my mouth. Do not forsake her, and she*
> *will keep you; love her, and she will guard*
> *you. The beginning of wisdom is this: Get*
> *wisdom, and whatever you get, get insight.*
> *Prize her highly, and she will exalt you; she*
> *will honor you if you embrace her. She will*
> *place on your head a graceful garland; she*
> *will bestow on you a beautiful crown."*
> *(Proverbs 4:5-9)*

Wisdom isn't something that just comes naturally, it's something that you have to intentionally pursue in your life. The best way to pursue wisdom is by pursuing the truths of God's Word. That means regular, personal Bible study and meditation. It means applying the principles of God's Word to daily living.

This is a process that we must never give up on. It is a lifelong process that we must be frequent and regular in. No one can say, "Well, I've gained all I can from God's Word." Every time we open the Bible we must be ready and listening for God's voice, because it is his very words that we are reading on every page. We must learn to value those truths and there is no better way to value them than by putting them to action in our lives.

The more familiar you become with God's Word, the easier it is for you to see how to apply Biblical principles to every area of your life. When you truly begin to seek wisdom from God's Word you will find that it touches every aspect of your life. It changes the way you think, it affects the choices you make at work, at home, at school, and even on vacation. It comes out in your speech, in your dress, in your spending,and in your attitude.

Regular and intentional study of God's Word will help you see those wisdom principles and apply them to your decision-making process. However, there is one more thing you can do to ensure that you are making wise choices, and that is simply to ask God for wisdom!

James instructs us to ask for wisdom.

> *If any of you lacks wisdom, let him ask*
> *God, who gives generously to all without*
> *reproach, and it will be given him.*
> *(James 1:5)*

Asking God for wisdom is an important step in gaining wisdom for two reasons. First, it acknowledges the truth that ultimately God is the source of all wisdom, and second, it humbly recognizes the fact that we are in desperate need of wisdom!

We tend to get hung up asking God for health or finances or strength to do our task, and those things are not wrong. However, God places a higher value on wisdom, and maybe it's because no matter what kind of help we need, wisdom is there to guide us.

When God told King Solomon that he could ask him for anything he desired, Solomon asked God for wisdom. This request pleased God so much, that he gave Solomon riches and honor, too! (1 Kings 3). If you ask God for wisdom you can be sure that he will give it!

QUESTION 3

HAVE YOU SOUGHT GODLY COUNCIL?

Making decisions on your own can be dangerous. The Bible often talks about the importance of seeking the council of godly people before making a decision. This doesn't mean simply getting the opinion of your friend or neighbor, but rather looking for a person who can accurately see your situation and shine the light of God's Word on it for you.

This can be especially helpful when the decision is particularly emotional for you. Emotions can cloud your thinking and make it difficult for you to see what Biblical principles are at play. Asking for the council of someone older and wiser is also a humbling thing to do. Just as asking God for wisdom indicates your own limits and inabilities, so also seeking guidance from another forces you to be humble, and that's a good thing!

Proverbs puts it this way.

> *The way of a fool is right in his own eyes,*
> *but a wise man listens to advice.*
> *(Proverbs 12:15)*

> *Where there is no guidance, a people*
> *falls, but in an abundance of counselors*
> *there is safety.*
> *(Pro 11:14)*

When you look for a person to give you Biblical advice, there are a few things to keep in mind. You should look for someone who has experience in life and a history of making wise choices. You should also look for someone who knows God's Word well and exhibits evidence that their Biblical knowledge has been applied to their lives. I suggests that you begin your search at your local church.

QUESTION 4

HAVE YOU PRAYED ABOUT IT?

This is the final question in my list, but that doesn't mean you have to wait until the end of the decision-making process to do it. In fact, it's a good idea to start the process with prayer, continue the process with prayer, and end it with prayer!

God wants us to acknowledge our dependence upon him by coming to him and asking for guidance in our decisions. Even if you feel fairly confident that you are making a good decision, it's a wise practice to pray about it before making it final. King David is a great example for us. He often turned to God in prayer before making a decision.

When David's men were worried and afraid to attack the Philistine army, David prayed and asked for guidance.

> *Now they told David, "Behold, the Philistines are fighting against Keilah and are robbing the threshing floors." Therefore David inquired of the LORD, "Shall I go and attack these Philistines?" And the LORD said to David, "Go and attack the Philistines and save Keilah." But David's men said to him, "Behold, we are afraid here in Judah; how much more then if we go to Keilah against the armies of the Philistines?" Then David inquired of the LORD again. And the LORD answered him, "Arise, go down to Keilah, for I will give the Philistines into your hand."*
> *(1 Samuel 23:1-4)*

That wasn't the only time David asked God for guidance. In the books of 1st and 2nd Samuel, David inquires of God no less than seven times!

NOW TRUST THE LORD!

Let's put it all together now.

- Is your decision righteous?
- Is your decision wise?
- Does your decision agree with godly council?
- Have your prayed about your decision?

132

If you can answer "yes" to all the questions above, then you're ready to move on, make your decision, and trust the Lord for the results! The fact is, there's really nothing more you can do. You've done what God requires of you. As long as the circumstances of your decision haven't changed, then you must step forward in faith and trust God to work things out.

Doubting your decision now is really nothing more than a lack of faith. It's not trusting that God can and will guide you, it's not believing that God does listen to your prayers, it's doubting that the Biblical principles on which your decision is based are really true.

Again we come back to Proverbs, the book of wisdom.

*Trust in the LORD with all your heart, and
do not lean on your own understanding. In
all your ways acknowledge him, and he will
make straight your paths.*
(Proverbs 3:5-6)

Honor God by putting your worry about your decision in his hands. In doing so, you allow yourself the opportunity to move on, to continue serving the Lord, and pursuing righteousness!

CHAPTER

17

KILL WORRY WITH GOD'S WORD

Worry fixes your mind on the theoretical and the possibility of unforeseen problems. Worry focuses on what you can't know, so if you want to get rid of it, the best thing you can do is turn your mind back to something you know is true beyond any doubt!

God's Word is a great worry killer because it brings us back to right thinking, it anchors our mind and heart in truth that will never change and in a God who knows our every problem and who can give us exactly what we need when we need it.

Reading the Bible isn't just another trick or a way to distract your mind long enough so that you forget about your worries. If you allow it, Bible reading will change the way you think and what you think about. When you combine a correct understanding of God's Word with a solid faith in the truth of those words, God will change your mind and your heart.

Look at how David describes the action of God's Word in our lives.

> *The law of the LORD is perfect, reviving*
> *the soul; the testimony of the LORD is*
> *sure, making wise the simple; the precepts*

of the LORD are right, rejoicing the heart;
the commandment of the LORD is pure,
enlightening the eyes;
(Psalm 19:7-8)

There are four promises here, God's Word can do the following:

- Revive your soul
- Make you wise
- Give you joy
- Enlighten your eyes

These are all qualities that can replace worry in your life! They represent a mind and a heart that has a proper focus. It is a mind that's directed by God's Word and a heart that is at peace because it has found true peace in the pages of Scripture.

Reading through this psalm and others you see more than the lack of worry, there's an overwhelming sense of peace, tranquility, and joy. These are all qualities that seem to be uncommon in today's world of chaos, turbulence, and anger. The truth is that many of these psalms were written during chaotic, stressful, and dangerous times for the author, yet despite the turmoil on the outside, he managed to find a sanctuary of peace on the inside.

Too often we think that if we could only find a calm and quiet setting, if only things were under control in our life, if only we didn't have such chaos around us, then we would have peace. What are we really doing when we think like that? We are allowing our outward circumstances to determine our inward state!

Yes, it's nice to get away to a peaceful spot and it can be healthy for us to do so from time to time. However, we need to realize that ultimately, true peace and freedom from worry does not come from a tranquil setting. Victory over worry must be firmly rooted in the truth of God's Word. This is a work only God can do as you read, understand, and apply the Bible to your thinking, your attitudes, and your actions!

Let's look again at the words of King David.

> *The sorrows of those who run after another god shall multiply; their drink offerings of blood I will not pour out or take their names on my lips. The LORD is my chosen portion and my cup; you hold my lot. The lines have fallen for me in pleasant places; indeed, I have a beautiful inheritance. I bless the LORD who gives me counsel; in the night also my heart instructs me. I have set the LORD always before me; because he is at my right hand, I shall not be shaken. Therefore my heart is glad, and my whole being rejoices; my flesh also dwells secure.*
> *(Psalm 16:4-9)*

David correctly sees the problems that exist in the lives of those who run after other gods. Because they have not chosen to pursue truth, they are not pursuing the true God. The result of not seeking the true God is sorrow multiplied!

When it comes down to it, choosing to read the Bible and to use it as the guide for your heart is really about choosing to seek God and to make him Lord of your life. The Bible is God's Word, it is God's voice, it is God's truth and instruction for man! In the Bible, we find out who God is and who we are; we are warned of mistakes we have not made and we learn of truths that will never change.

David calls this pursuit of God "pleasant" and "beautiful." Notice also that his quest for God wasn't an insignificant hobby, thoughtless routine, or tedious duty. David blesses the Lord for his instruction and counsel, he also indicates that his pursuit of God is so encompassing, that it instructs him at night and he claims that the Lord is always at his right hand.

It is clear that David pursued God with his whole being, he gave himself to this pursuit, and thus it affected every aspect of his life. It directed his thought life, influenced his decisions, and gave him a rock-solid foundation of faith that left him feeling secure, cheerful, and confident!

Outside of God and his Word there is nothing in the world that can give you what David had! Nature can't provide it, money can't purchase it, and medications can't manufacture it! The peace and confidence that you and I and every living soul longs for must supersede our surroundings, be deeper than our problems, and stronger than our struggles.

God's Word provides us with eternal qualities based on unchanging truths. It points us to real solutions that transform our thinking and revolutionize our heart! It's ability to change us is not dependant upon our situation, but upon God's power to work in our hearts and change us from the inside out.

MAKE IT A HABIT

Whether you've never read the Bible before, you're just getting started, or you've been doing it for many years, I want to give you a few suggestions that will help make your Bible-reading truly meaningful in your life.

If we are not careful, Bible-reading can become another chore, another ritual, another thing to check off our list, and to make us feel spiritual and like we've fulfilled our debt to God. So let me start by telling you this - there is no Bible verse that says you must read the Bible every day, there's no verse that says you have to read through the Bible in a year, there's no verse that says you have to read early in the morning or late at night or at lunch!

However, there are many verses that speak about the value of reading, studying, and meditating on God's Word. Just read Psalm 1, Psalm 19, and Psalm 119!

There are also many verses that speak of the power and ability of God's Word to change our lives and guide our steps. Just read

Matthew 4:4, 1 Timothy 3:16-17, and Hebrews 4:12!

So when I talk about reading your Bible daily, it's not because God has somewhere commanded us to read our Bible every morning, but rather because it is a wise and good thing to do. Reading your Bible every day is one of the best habits you can establish because it ensures that your mind intakes a healthy dose of truth on a regular basis.

SET A TIME

Find a time in the day that generally works well for you. Maybe you're a morning person and that's the best time for you to open up God's Word with a nice cup of coffee. Maybe you're a night owl and you'd rather dig into God's Word long after everyone else has gone to sleep. Maybe you have a nice quiet spot in the middle of your day when you can study. The time of day doesn't matter, what matters is that it works for you!

READ THE INTRODUCTIONS

Many people tend to overlook this step, but it can really make a big difference in how much you understand as you begin a new book of the Bible.

What I'm talking about is the two or three page introductions to each book of the Bible that you might find in the NIV Study Bible or The MacArthur Study Bible. Obviously, these aren't inspired, but they do help us understand things like the history, cultural setting, main themes, and author of each book.

READ LONGER SECTIONS

There are many good reading plans out there that will guide you through the Bible in a year, and that's great. I honestly think a reading plan can be very helpful. However, most reading plans have you reading three to five chapters each day, and most books of the Bible weren't really meant to be read that way.

Consider this, the Book of Acts has about 18,000 words in most English translations. The average adult reads about 250 words a minute. That means you could read through the entire book of Acts in less time than it takes you to watch a movie!

I suggests from time to time you sit down, and read through an entire book of the Bible in one sitting. You may want to start with a shorter book like Ephesians or Colossians. You'll find this practice to be very beneficial, as it helps you understand the whole of the book, not just the parts.

READ ALOUD OR LISTEN

I can't overstate how much I love to listen to the Bible! Even Paul says that "faith comes by hearing." Most of the Bible was designed to be read aloud. It was a practice in the Jewish synagogues to read the Law aloud to the congregation. Ezra read the entire book of the Law to the people of Israel after they returned from captivity. (Nehemiah 8:1-8) Jesus read a section from the Prophet Isaiah aloud when he was in Jerusalem. (Luke 4:17-18) Paul also exhorted Timothy to publicly read the Scriptures. (1 Timothy 4:13)

There is something about hearing God's Word that is different than reading silently. If you are an audible learner, like me, then you know that often you understand better and retain things longer if you hear them. Even if you don't consider yourself to be an audible learner, I think it's worth trying from time to time.

LISTEN WHILE YOU'RE DOING SOMETHING ELSE

One of the greatest advantages of listening to Bible audio is that you can listen while you do other things. This may sound odd, but, it works. Don't think that you have to sit in a chair with your

Bible in your lap while listening to your audio Bible, although you can if you want to! There is scientific evidence that says our brains are able to assimilate information better when our bodies are busy doing something else. Sometimes I like to listen while I'm doing the dishes, vacuuming, walking, or even working out!

ASK THE RIGHT QUESTIONS

If you don't ask questions while reading, then you're really not engaging your mind! Here are few good questions to start with:

- Who is the main character?
- What main problem is this text addressing?
- Who was this written to?
- What does this teach me about God's character?
- What principles can I apply to my life?

Those should get you started, but feel free to add more, a lot more!

RE-READ

Sometimes we need to forget about our Bible reading plan and stop and re-read, once, twice, as many times as we need. I often re-read a text dozens of times every day in preparation for preaching. It gives the mind time to process, and the results can be amazing!

APPLY WHAT YOU'VE LEARNED

Without real life application, your Bible reading will do you more harm than good! The more you ignore the truth of Scripture, the easier it becomes to read a text and completely miss how it applies to your life. Your goal in Bible reading should not be "to get it done," but rather to understand truth and apply it to your life.

You need God's Word in the depths of your heart where it hurts a bit and makes you squirm. You need truth that gets between your fingers when you work, that slides off your tongue when you speak, principles that are embedded into the fiber of your being. You need God's Word to change you and that means you're going to have to put the Word of God into action in your life.

James gives a clear warning here.

> *But be doers of the word, and not hearers only, deceiving yourselves. For if anyone is a hearer of the word and not a doer, he is like a man who looks intently at his natural face in a mirror. For he looks at himself and goes away and at once forgets what he was like. But the one who looks into the perfect law, the law of liberty, and perseveres, being no hearer who forgets but a doer who acts, he will be blessed in his doing.*
> *(James 1:22-25)*

If you're going to be a doer of God's and not just a hearer, then you must not forget the truths that you have learned in your reading. Those truths must work their way out in your every day life!

Here are a few suggestions for making God's Word apply to your life.

1. Before you read, ask God to open your eyes to how the truths you will read affect your life in specific ways.
2. When you read, look for good examples to follow and bad examples to avoid.
3. When you read, ask yourself what the text reveals about the character of God.
4. When you read, look for specific commands like "Do not commit adultery" or "Love the Lord your God."
5. After you read, spend a few minutes in prayer and meditation and ask God to help you apply what you've read to your life.
6. After you read, write down any key truths you've

142

learned, decisions you've made or questions you have.

Reading your bible isn't just another trick to help you stop worrying. It is a life-giving source of truth that will change you from the inside out. Once you find yourself looking into God's Word regularly and intently, you will quickly see how God can change your thinking, change your mind, and change your heart. It is this transformation power coming only from God's Word which will ultimately kill your worry, anxiety, and fear.

KILL WORRY WITH PRAYER

I grew up in a pastor's family and that means I heard a lot of prayers growing up. I remember going to prayer meetings as a young boy; it was probably one of the most boring things I could think of at the time. After a few songs, we would break up into groups of half a dozen or so. There we would sit huddled up in a circle and share a few more prayer requests. Then it would start, theological expositions of God's greatness, his ability, his power, and so on.

I remember sitting there when I was about six years old, struggling to keep my head from falling between my knees and my body from sliding off the chair as I wavered in and out of consciousness. After a few minutes I'd jerk my head up involuntarily and then wonder if I'd been sleeping for long or if anyone had noticed!

What really amazed me was how people changed their vocabulary the moment they began to pray. It was almost like they were praying in tongues, but I knew they weren't because it was a baptist church! There were a few people in particular that I dreaded. I would watch as they prayed around the circle, things would be moving along at a decent pace. I even timed some of them!

The average church member could go for two or three minutes.

The committed church member would be closer to five minutes. Then there was the ultra committed, the one that put everyone else to shame. He would take five minutes just for his introduction! He couldn't get into the body of his prayer until he completed a full dissertation on the holiness and greatness of God using every theological term in his arsenal!

The truth is that we often learn to pray by listening to others pray. That's why, as a child, I thought good prayers must use a healthy amount of "thees" and "thous," and it never hurts to throw in a few well accepted biblical cliches.

As I grew in my faith I began to realize that a lot of what I was seeing and hearing wasn't the best example of prayer. Thanks to some bad examples, I learned what prayer is not!

- Prayer is not simply a list of needs you dictate to God.
- Prayer is not mindless repetition of memorized text.
- Prayer is not a psychological exercise to strengthen the mind or channel your energy.
- Prayer is not a magical incantation that forces God to do what you want.

Prayer is none of the things listed above, and the sooner you understand that, the sooner you'll be able to correctly grasp what prayer is and therefore engage in it.

Simply put, prayer is talking to God. It is our response to a righteous and good God. It is our cry for help, our humble acknowledgement of our need for forgiveness, our thankfulness, our praise, and adoration. It is an ongoing conversation with our all-knowing Heavenly Father. It is talking through all the issues of life with the one person who knows us best and loves us the most.

Prayer is essential for your spiritual life, and it is one of our greatest tools to kill worry and anxiety. Yet, we often forget to pray or even avoid it! Why is this?

SIN KEEPS US FROM PRAYING

Let's take a look at the first prayer ever recorded. You may be thinking that the first prayer is most likely some sort of amazing and beautifully put together sonnet of praise and adoration of God. Well, if that's what you thought, then you're quite mistaken!

You see the first prayer in the Bible took place in the Garden of Eden after Adam and Eve sinned against God. Later when they heard God walking in the garden, they hid themselves out of shame for what they had done. They were worried that God would find out. They were afraid of what might happen to them when God saw they had eaten from the Tree of the Knowledge of Good and Evil.

When God called for them Adam responded by saying,

> *I heard the sound of you in the garden,*
> *and I was afraid, because I was naked,*
> *and I hid myself.*
> *(Genesis 3:10)*

Wow! So that's it? That's the first recorded prayer? It doesn't seem too theological or impressive, does it? That's because it's not! It's simply Adam honestly confessing his problem to God, and that's the absolute best thing he could do at that time.

To tell you the truth, I'm glad Adam didn't give God some sort of sophisticated theological answer. He didn't start talking about original sin and how it was all God's plan anyway, and he was really helping God out, because if he hadn't sinned, then Jesus could never become the Savior of the world, and this would really make God look good in the long run, and on and on...

God wasn't looking for Adam to impress him with his deep theological insight. He was simply looking for Adam to humbly confess his sin and ask for forgiveness! And that's where prayer must always start! Without a humble spirit, without the understanding that you have messed up and you need forgiveness that only God can offer, prayer cannot take place!

The problem we face is this, sin always draws us away from God. As a result of the first sin, Adam and Eve went into hiding, they didn't want to talk to God or to even see him. The sound of God walking in the garden was enough to make them turn on their heels and run! So at our most desperate time and the time when we have our greatest need to talk to God, we are often torn from him by our own sin.

A few years ago, one of my girls, who was about two years old at the time, secretly stole her mother's lipstick and began to apply it. Later, she emerged from the bathroom with a thick burgundy stripe halfway across her face. It wasn't difficult for us as parents to tell what happened. She had broken the rules by getting into her mother's make-up bag. The evidence was literally written all over her face!

Now here's the ironic part! I confronted her while she was still holding the open tube of lipstick in her hand and asked her directly, "Did you use Mama's lipstick?" Her response? She looked at me with eyes about to water over with tears and said, "No, I was just looking at it!" Although I knew the truth from looking at her face, I wanted to hear it from her, I wanted her to confess the truth! The problem was that her guilt kept her from doing what she needed to do; confess her sin and ask for forgiveness.

Unfortunately, we often do the same thing. When life gets tough, when problems multiply, we rarely think of our need for help, of the importance of confessing our problems and our faults to God and acknowledging our dependence upon him alone! This, however, is exactly what God wants us to do, only God doesn't want us to wait until we've run out of options and there's no where else to turn. He wants us to turn and talk to him now.

PRAYER IS CONFESSION

The prophet Daniel in the Old Testament was committed to prayer, and as a result, God did some amazing things through him. It was a time in Israel's history when they had completely turned away from God. Daniel realized the need to turn back and confess the sins that were pulling them away from God. Here is how he addressed God in prayer:

> *Then I turned my face to the Lord God, seeking him by prayer and pleas for mercy with fasting and sackcloth and ashes. I prayed to the LORD my God and made confession, saying, "O Lord, the great and awesome God, who keeps covenant and steadfast love with those who love him and keep his commandments, we have sinned and done wrong and acted wickedly and rebelled, turning aside from your commandments and rules."*
> *(Daniel 9:3-5)*

Daniel's prayer is a great example for us. If we want to deal with the problem of worry in our lives, we must start by realizing that it truly is a sin, and confessing it to God. Then we must make it a practice of coming to God in prayer before the worry even starts!

PRAYER IS CONVERSATION WITH GOD

One of the most important aspects about prayer that I have learned is that prayer should be an ongoing conversation between you and God. The Apostle Paul simply states it like this:

> *Pray without ceasing.*
> *(1Thessalonians 5:17)*

Have you ever wondered how that could be done? At first glance, it seems like Paul is asking us to close ourselves up in a room somewhere and spend all day and night on our knees doing nothing but praying silently. Is that even possible? Wouldn't you eventually run out of things to pray about? Don't you have to live life, too?

Thankfully, that's not really what Paul is asking us to do. He doesn't want you to stop going to work or stop taking care of your children or stop going to birthday parties or stop spending time with your family so that you can do nothing but pray. In fact, Paul isn't asking you to disengage from life at all, but rather to engage with the ultimate source of life. He's asking you to interact with the life-giver on a continual basis as you live the life he gave you.

We all carry on conversations in our heads as we go about our daily tasks. Sometimes that conversation is so active that I wake up in the morning with words swirling in my head like storm clouds. Before I get out of bed I'm already talking to myself about plans for the day, things I need to get done, decisions that need to be made.

Sometimes I'll recall a conversation I had with someone and begin analyzing it and wondering why they said this or I said that! Sometimes there's a particular problem with one of the kids and I'm talking to myself about how to deal with it. Often I'm thinking about a sermon I need to prepare or a report I need to write, and it all happens in my head throughout the day as I talk to myself.

Now lets bring worry and anxiety into the picture. When you worry, you will find that worry starts to permeate that ongoing conversation in your head. Worry invades your thinking and inserts itself into the thought process. Instead of planning for today's activity, you begin to think about the ways that it could go wrong. Instead of deciding how to respond to a difficult situation, you begin to stress over how people will think of you. Instead of turning to God and asking for help to pay the bills, you begin to worry about where the money will come from!

Worry is like an invasive species of plant that sends its tendrils down into the soil of your mind and touches everything you think about, everything you talk about, everything you do! But what if you could change all that? What if you could exchange the invasiveness of worry for permeation with prayer?

You can! That's exactly what Paul is talking about when he says "Pray without ceasing." He's telling us that we need to make that on-going conversation in our heads a conversation that includes God! What would happen in your life right now if you exchanged all your worry with prayer? It would make a difference, wouldn't it?

So why not do it? Exchange your constant worry with prayer! Don't just push anxiety out of your mind, replace it with a constant conversation with God! When worry sends it's life-sucking roots into the middle of your thought life, use it as a reminder to pray without ceasing. Don't let worry get by in your mind for more than a second without turning to God and giving it to him. Take Paul's advice to the Philippians.

> *Do not be anxious about anything, but in everything by prayer and supplication with thanksgiving let your requests be made known to God.*
> *(Philippians 4:6)*

PRAYER IS THANKSGIVING

I find it interesting that when Paul talks about anxiety and prayer in Philippians 4:6, he also includes the idea of thanksgiving. I haven't heard anyone talk about the connection between thanksgiving and anxiety before, but they are certainly connected!

You can kill worry with prayer as you confess your sins to God and receive his forgiveness. You can also kill worry with prayer as you seek to replace worried thoughts with prayer and develop a continual conversation with God throughout your day. Thanksgiving is the final part to this prayer puzzle.

It's not really enough just to pray and ask God for his help, we must do more. We must acknowledge the help he has already given us, we must communicate our gratefulness for how he has already provided for our needs, protected us, and given us many blessings that we don't deserve!

How does giving thanks kill worry? Simply by changing the way we think and putting our hearts into right relation with God. You see, once you come to terms with God's great care and concern for you, once you understand the scope of his gracious provision for you, it is nearly impossible to worry! If you have come to that realization without giving thanks, then you're robbing God of glory that only he deserves!

Earlier I talked about I Thessalonians 5:17, where Paul tells us "Pray without ceasing." Do you know what he says in the next verse? Yes, that's right, he talks about giving thanks!

Give thanks in all circumstances; for this is
the will of God in Christ Jesus for you.
(1Thessalonians 5:18)

I've never met a truly grateful person who also struggles with worry and anxiety. The truth is that worry can not coexist with a heart that is overflowing with gratitude towards God. Thankfulness is the knowledge that God has provided and will continue to provide. Thankfulness is the belief that God is still ultimately in control. Thankfulness is giving God his rightly deserved praise for sticking with us in the toughest times and the greatest pain. Thankfulness acknowledges the fact that we really have nothing to worry about if God is on our side!

19

KILL WORRY WITH MEMORY AND MEDITATION

In chapter seventeen, we looked at the importance of reading and studying God's Word as a way to overcome worry. We discussed how to make that a meaningful and regular part of your life. In this final chapter, I want to look at two other aspects which are related to Scripture.

Bible memory and meditation are both tools that you can use to refine God's Word in your heart and mind and to ensure that it permeates every aspect of your life. You can think of Bible reading and study like eating. It's vital to your life, you will not grow or survive long unless you are continually ingesting nutritious food. But it's not enough simply get the food from your plate and into your mouth. After the food enters your mouth is must be chewed, swallowed, and digested before it can really do it's job of providing your body with the nutrients it needs.

Bible memory and meditation perform the function of chewing and digestion in our mind and heart. They take what we have read and studied in God's Word, and put it through a process. That process is important, because without it we often gain little to no benefit from reading the Bible.

If you're like me, you've probably had mornings when you read the Bible, stood up, and completely forgot everything you just read! If someone asked you thirty minutes later, you wouldn't have the faintest clue about what you read! When that happens, you can be sure that you're not getting what you need out of God's Word!

Memorization and meditation really go well together; it's almost difficult to have one without the other! Memorization is the discipline of learning and reciting texts of Scripture by heart word for word! Meditation is the discipline of focused, intentional thinking about a specific text or teaching of Scripture. They go together well because memorization is the catalyst our mind needs for meditation. In other words, memorization most naturally leads to meditation.

MEMORIZATION

There seems to be a misconception out there that only children should memorize things! Often Sunday School programs will have verses to memorize with rewards for those who accomplish it, but it seems like somewhere around high-school level the memorization stops.

Maybe it's because as adults we have so much information competing for space in our brain that we figure trying to memorize Scripture is useless. The truth is that the more information we have coming at us, the more important it is that we focus our mind on God's Word by memorizing key passages!

A couple of years ago I realized that my kids were memorizing lots of Bible verses in their school and I was doing nothing! Why should I expect them to learn all those verses while I sit back and relax? So I decided to do some memorizing myself. What I thought would be a laborious and tiresome activity turned into one of the most exciting things I'd done in a long time!

154

I knew that it would be good for me to memorize Scripture, but the process of learning God's Word by heart also taught me a few things that I didn't realize before.

IT CLEARS THE MIND

Do you ever have a hard time hard time shutting you mind off? Maybe it's the result of living in the age of information, or maybe it's the result of worrying too much; either way, there are things that get stuck in your head, things that you shouldn't continually dwell on. At those times, working on Scripture memory completely clears your mind. It forces everything else out and brings God's Word in. This is refreshing and relaxing to the mind at the same time!

IT CENTERS THE SPIRIT

You probably have those days too, when your emotions are off, you're grumpy or anxious and you don't want to do the things you know you should do. Sometimes I can't even pinpoint why I am feeling that way, but when I turn to Scripture and start filling my mind with it's truths, everything changes! Joy returns and passion is regained!

IT GIVES A FRESH PERSPECTIVE

When you're tackling a problem that you're just not sure how to resolve, it can be overwhelming. It's easy to get lost in the problem. The more you bury yourself into the situation and try to figure it out, the more difficult it can become to have proper perspective. Often a ten minute break to work on Scripture memory is all you need. You'll come back renewed and with a fresh perspective!

IT LEADS TO CORRECT THINKING

Thought habits are important; they determine how we are going to think about everything in our life, and thus how we will behave. Memorizing Scripture is one of the best thought habits we can promote in our mind. Not only does it strengthen the mind and make it more agile, but it also helps us develop correct thoughts about every area of life.

It Gives You 24/7 Access to God's Word

The written Word is great. You can hold it in your hand, read it on your couch, in your bed, or at your desk. It's versatile, but it can't be with you 24/7. There are times when, for practical reasons, you can't pick it up and read it. For instance, I don't suggest that you try reading the Bible while driving down the freeway, or while you're operating a table saw! That's a recipe for disaster!

Yet, any piece of God's Word that you have memorized you have access to 24/7 no matter what you're doing. You can recall those words in your head while you're in the shower, while driving to work, or in a crisis moment. It's there and ready to go, you don't have to search for a Bible or look up a reference, because you have God's Word in your mind!

TIPS ON MEMORIZING

If you're worried about memorizing being too difficult for you, I want to ensure you that you can do it! If you know a phone number by heart or the words of a song or the names of half a dozen people, then you can memorize something!

I suggest that you start small by learning a verse or two and then slowly expand the amount of text you are memorizing. The key to memorizing is not necessarily spending a lot of time at once, but spending a few minutes here and there throughout the day reviewing the verses you are working on. For instance, if you can consistently review your text three times a day for a week, you'll have no problem getting it memorized. The key is to be regular and consistent.

Try to use times to memorize when you are doing other things. I like to memorize while I walk to and from work. I print out a sheet with the text that I'm working on, and as I walk I review it as many times as I can before I get to work.

You may also want to consider working on memory verses at other times during the day. Use down times at work or times when you are waiting for someone to show up for a meeting. If you think about it, we all have times during our day that we could utilize for Scripture memory.

- Doing the dishes
- Cleaning the house
- Working out
- Commuting
- Walking
- Eating lunch
- Riding on the bus
- Waiting in line

MEDITATION

Let's be honest, we don't often hear about the importance of Biblical meditation. Maybe it's because the world of Yoga and Eastern Mysticism has stolen it from us. Usually when I talk about meditation, people have a picture in their head of a robed monk sitting in what looks like an uncomfortable pose with eyes closed and body motionless for hours at a time.

To be clear, that's not what I'm talking about! Unlike Eastern mysticism, which concentrates on emptying the mind, Biblical meditation is about focusing and filling your mind with God's Word! Its goal is to take a deeper look into God's Word by tuning it over and over again in your mind! Its aim is to move beyond understanding the meaning of the text and begin to see how it applies to every aspect of life! Its purpose is to integrate the truth of God's Word so deeply into the fabric of your soul, that your entire life becomes an expression of those truths!

Joshua said it best when he challenged the people of Israel to commit to living according to the standard set in Scripture.

> *This Book of the Law shall not depart from*
> *your mouth, but you shall meditate on it*
> *day and night, so that you may be careful*
> *to do according to all that is written in it.*
> *For then you will make your way prosper-*
> *ous, and then you will have good success.*
> *(Joshua 1:8)*

Joshua called on the people to meditate on the Book of the Law (Scripture) day and night! Why was this important? So that they would be careful to obey it! Life application is the main purpose behind Biblical meditation.

Biblical meditation is to worry as water is to fire. If you want to get rid of your worry and anxiety in a hurry, then grab yourself a bucket of God's Word and douse your mind with it. Let it fill every nook and cranny, let it seep into the deepest parts of your soul, let it quench the fire of anxiety and cool your troubled mind!

Yes, meditation can get rid of worry in a hurry but it's the consistent disciplined practice of meditation that produces the greatest and most lasting results in our lives!

So how do you practice Biblical meditation? Is there a preferred position? Do you need to find a room with the right feng shui? Do you need music or a special robe?

You need none of those things, although you could use them if you wanted! Biblical meditation simply requires God's Word in your mind and the discipline to focus your attention on it.

There are two types of meditation that I practice. The first is focused, undistributed, silent meditation. For this type of meditation you'll want to choose a quiet place where you'll not be disturbed. I often do this when I am preparing to preach. After I have spent sufficient time studying the text, I will simply close my eyes and silently think about it! I'll ask myself questions about personal application and I will also quietly pray in response to the truths I am learning.

On a few occasions, my wife has come into the room while I'm meditating and thought I was asleep. But I wasn't, in fact my mind is probably more actively engaged when I meditate then when I'm doing anything else. The key is that the engagement is focused and free of distraction.

Usually after a time of meditation, I'll jot down my thoughts on a piece of paper or on my computer so that I don't forget the things that God's Word brought to my mind.

The second type of meditation is ongoing, it can be done at any time during the day. It takes advantage of that background conversation that is going on in your head as you clean your house, drive to work, or mow the lawn. If whatever you're doing doesn't take focused mental effort, then you can focus your mind on the truths of God's Word while your busy with your task.

What this means for me is that I can use the twenty-five minutes it takes me to walk to work. I also often focus my mind on God's Word while I'm exercising. Using times like this throughout the day to meditate on God's Word is a discipline and a skill that must be developed.

The point of this type of meditation isn't so that the only thing we ever think about is God's Word, but rather so that everything we think about is affected by God's Word! This can only happen as we develop the habit of regular meditation throughout the day.

No chapter in the Bible speaks more directly and more often about the importance of meditation than Psalm 119. In this

Psalm, David describes his great love and passion for God's Word. He talks about its ability to guide his steps and protect his life. He also shows us how meditation on God's Word must infiltrate our daily lives.

*Oh how I love your law! It is my
meditation all the day.*
(Psalm 119:97)

When you exchange your worry and anxiety for meditation on God's Word, you will find a whole new life open up for you. You'll do much more than eliminate worry from your life, you'll find out what true joy and peace are! Your life will become an example of God's power and leading. You're desires and habits will change, your hopes and dreams will begin to reflect Biblical truths, and your passions will be directed by God instead of by your fears!

WHAT IT LOOKS LIKE

What does this look like in real life? In Psalm one, the writer describes the life of a man who is consumed with God's Word and has made it his pursuit and joy in life.

*Blessed is the man who walks not in the
counsel of the wicked, nor stands in the
way of sinners, nor sits in the seat of
scoffers; but his delight is in the law of the
LORD, and on his law he meditates day and
night. He is like a tree planted by streams
of water that yields its fruit in its season,
and its leaf does not wither. In all that he
does, he prospers.*
(Psalm 1:1-3)

What we see here is a beautiful picture of a man who meditates on God's Word day and night. Notice the difference it has made in his life! It affects his choices, it brings him delight, and he is called a blessed man! He is well-rooted and he produces is fruit!

Key to this whole psalm is the fact that the blessed man has chosen to delight in God's law and meditate on it day and night! That's what has made the difference in his life, that's why he is careful not to be influenced by, and take the advice of, those who do not respect God's Word. That's why he will eventually produce good fruit in his life and that's why he is called blessed!

Worry robs us of joy and often keeps us from recognizing the blessings God is giving us! The man described in this text seems to know that he is blessed. He even experiences delight as he meditates on God's Word. While the text doesn't specifically refer to worry, it paints a picture of a man who knows God so well, that he is disturbed by nothing. He is boldly living with his roots sunk deep into the soil of God's Word! He knows that his future is secure because of the promises he has read in Scripture.

YOU CAN KILL WORRY!

You too can live like this man! You can kill worry, be filled with joy, and confident in the future! There's really no secret to it, there's no hidden button to push or little-known trick to relieve you of your worry. Killing worry is a process that must start with a step of faith. It begins with trust in God's Word, which is really trust in God himself!

The journey begins with God's Word and continues every day as you make the decision to dig deeper, learn more, and trust God in ways you have never trusted him before! It's a journey that will take a lifetime. A lifetime of removing fear, doubt, and apprehension from every corner of your heart! A lifetime of filling the voids in your soul with God's Word, with prayer, with thanksgiving, and praise! A lifetime of learning who God is and watching him work in every facet of your being.

HELPFUL SCRIPTURES

In peace I will both lie down and sleep; for you alone, O LORD, make me dwell in safety.
(Psalm 4:8)

Even though I walk through the valley of the shadow of death, I will fear no evil, for you are with me; your rod and your staff, they comfort me. You prepare a table before me in the presence of my enemies; you anoint my head with oil; my cup overflows. Surely goodness and mercy shall follow me all the days of my life, and I shall dwell in the house of the LORD forever.
(Psalm 23:4-6)

Cast your burden on the LORD, and he will sustain you; he will never permit the righteous to be moved.
(Psalm 55:22)

To the choirmaster. A Psalm of David. O LORD, you have searched me and known me! You know when I sit down and when I rise up; you discern my thoughts from afar. You search out my path and my lying down and are acquainted with all my ways. Even before a word is on my tongue, behold, O LORD, you know it altogether. You hem me in, behind and before, and lay your hand upon me. Such knowledge is too wonderful for me; it is high; I cannot attain it. Where shall I go from your Spirit? Or where shall I flee from your presence? If I ascend to heaven, you are there! If I make my bed in Sheol, you are there! If I take the wings of the morning and dwell in the uttermost parts of the sea, even there your hand shall lead me, and your right hand shall

hold me. If I say, "Surely the darkness shall cover me, and the light about me be night," even the darkness is not dark to you; the night is bright as the day, for darkness is as light with you. For you formed my inward parts; you knitted me together in my mother's womb.
(Psalm 139:1-13)

Look at the birds of the air: they neither sow nor reap nor gather into barns, and yet your heavenly Father feeds them. Are you not of more value than they? And which of you by being anxious can add a single hour to his span of life? And why are you anxious about clothing? Consider the lilies of the field, how they grow: they neither toil nor spin, yet I tell you, even Solomon in all his glory was not arrayed like one of these. But if God so clothes the grass of the field, which today is alive and tomorrow is thrown into the oven, will he not much more clothe you, O you of little faith? Therefore do not be anxious, saying, 'What shall we eat?' or 'What shall we drink?' or 'What shall we wear?' For the Gentiles seek after all these things, and your heavenly Father knows that you need them all. But seek first the kingdom of God and his righteousness, and all these things will be added to you. "Therefore do not be anxious about tomorrow, for tomorrow will be anxious for itself. Sufficient for the day is its own trouble.
(Matthew 6:26-34)

And he said to his disciples, "Therefore I tell you, do not be anxious about your life, what you will eat, nor about your body, what you will put on. For life is more than food, and the body more than clothing. Consider the ravens: they neither sow nor reap, they have neither storehouse nor barn, and yet God feeds them. Of how much more value are you than the birds! And which of you by being anxious can add a single hour to his span of life? If then you are not able to do as small a thing as that, why are you anxious about the rest? Consider the lilies, how they grow: they neither toil nor spin, yet I tell you, even Solomon in all his glory was not arrayed like one of these. But if God so clothes the grass, which is alive in the field today, and tomorrow is thrown into the oven, how much more will he clothe you, O you of little faith! And do not seek what you are to eat and what you are to drink,

nor be worried. For all the nations of the world seek after these things, and your Father knows that you need them. Instead, seek his kingdom, and these things will be added to you.
(**Luke 12:22-31**)

But Martha was distracted with much serving. And she went up to him and said, "Lord, do you not care that my sister has left me to serve alone? Tell her then to help me." But the Lord answered her, "Martha, Martha, you are anxious and troubled about many things, but one thing is necessary. Mary has chosen the good portion, which will not be taken away from her."
(**Luke 10:40-42**)

"But watch yourselves lest your hearts be weighed down with dissipation and drunkenness and cares of this life, and that day come upon you suddenly like a trap.
(**Luke 21:34**)

Do not be anxious about anything, but in everything by prayer and supplication with thanksgiving let your requests be made known to God. And the peace of God, which surpasses all understanding, will guard your hearts and your minds in Christ Jesus. Finally, brothers, whatever is true, whatever is honorable, whatever is just, whatever is pure, whatever is lovely, whatever is commendable, if there is any excellence, if there is anything worthy of praise, think about these things.
(**Philippians 4:6-8**)

Humble yourselves, therefore, under the mighty hand of God so that at the proper time he may exalt you, casting all your anxieties on him, because he cares for you.
(**1 Peter 5:6-7**)

ABOUT THE AUTHOR

Since 2007 Caleb has served as a missionary in Odessa, Ukraine where he is pastor at Hope for People Church and director of "Evangelism Today" center for evangelism and discipleship. http://blagovestie.today. Caleb attended Shasta Bible College and graduated from North West Baptist seminary in 2005 with a Masters of Divinity.

Together with his wife Christina their desire is to help believers and churches to do biblical evangelism and discipleship. This is accomplished by conducting training seminars on evangelism and discipleship for churches. It also involves personal discipleship and working closely with national pastors to help strengthen and multiply the Church in Ukraine and beyond.

The Sukos have five children.

If you'd like to learn more about the Suko's ministry please visit http://sukofamily.org

For questions or comments about the book please visit http://sukofamily.org/whatif

Made in the USA
Coppell, TX
27 May 2020